Diploma Diaries

THE CHIC GRAD'S GUIDE TO WORK, LOVE, AND EVERYTHING IN BETWEEN

Christie Garton

This publication is designed to provide accurate and authoritative information in regard to the subject matter covered. It is sold with the understanding that the publisher is not engaged in rendering legal, accounting, or other professional service. If legal advice or other expert assistance is required, the services of a competent professional person should be sought.—*From a Declaration of Principles Jointly Adopted by a Committee of the American Bar Association and a Committee of Publishers and Associations*

Published by Sourcebooks, Inc.
P.O. Box 4410, Naperville, Illinois 60567-4410
(630) 961-3900
Fax: (630) 961-2168
www.sourcebooks.com

Library of Congress Cataloging-in-Publication Data

Garton, Christie.
U chic's diploma diaries : the chic grad's guide to work, love, and everything in between / Christie Garton.
pages cm
1. Young women—Life skills guide. 2. College graduates—Life skills guide. 3. College graduates—Employment. 4. School-to-work transition. I. Title.
HQ799.5.G37 2013
305.242'2—dc23

2013001721

Printed and bound in the United States of America.
VP 10 9 8 7 6 5 4 3 2 1

To the women of UChic.com,
the true inspiration behind this book.

contents

introduction

Congratulations! If you're reading this book, then you have succeeded or are very close to succeeding in completing what are arguably the best four years of your life. (But you know what? We think the best is yet to come.) In any case, graduating from college is a significant accomplishment that should not to be taken lightly, and you should be proud.

Despite the sense of pride you have rightfully earned, you may also be feeling a little uneasy. That is completely normal. Reaching the end of one's college career brings a mixed bag of emotions for every graduate, even those who appear to have everything figured out. On one hand, it's thrilling not to have to write another term paper or cram for a test you are oh-so-not prepared for. On the other, the stress over the future and "what comes next"—on top of officially becoming a full-fledged adult—is a lot to have to suddenly take on.

Plus, these days, you're facing a whole new set of challenges that do not have easy answers. From a lack of high-quality jobs for recent college grads to the crushing burden of student-loan debt, we could all use some sound advice on how best to navigate the transition from college to the ever-more-challenging real world.

That is what *Diploma Diaries* is all about. Because you've lived long enough to know more or less what works for you, we decided against writing just another how-to guide. Instead, we approached the experts—young women like yourself who are dealing with the very same issues you are—and asked them to share their personal stories on how they managed the postcollege transition.

After college, I often found that the best advice came through "how I did it" stories from older friends and mentors. Consider our book's contributors your mentors—girls you can grab your favorite coffee drink with while you dig into their "how I did it" guidance. In addition to their stories—some that may make you laugh and others that might shock you with their raw honesty—we've included advice, tips, and tricks throughout the book as "U Chic's Reality Check" boxes that are designed specifically to help you navigate this challenging time.

That said, with *U Chic's Diploma Diaries*, the conversation doesn't stop at the last page. Let's say you have a specific question that is not directly addressed in this book. Visit www.UChic.com/Diploma-Diaries where you can ask your question, interact with other readers, and share your own tips. This guide is really the start of a conversation that can last throughout your twenties and into your thirties.

That's *Diploma Diaries* in a nutshell. So read on and get inspired as you move forward with your fabulous future. After all, it's yours to create, so go out and make of it what you want!

xoxo,
Christie Garton
Founder and Publisher,
UChic.com

CHAPTER 1

Real World Bound

So you're getting set to graduate from college. Or maybe you already have. You're likely wondering what your future holds. Great question, right? That's entirely your call. As the saying goes, the sky is the limit.

But hold on a sec! While it's inspiring to think that the future holds limitless possibilities with the right experience in your back pocket (like that hard-won diploma), it is frustrating that the specifics on how to accomplish those possibilities—what to focus on and what steps to take—aren't readily apparent.

The reality is that while you have been on a long journey to get that college degree, it is far from over. Your journey into the real world brings a whole new set of challenges not seen during college, and with these challenges come incredible possibilities. The main difference between the college and the real-world journeys is the heightened focus on your sense of self. The postcollege transition is truly a time for self-discovery.

In the real world, you no longer have a professor or academic advisor to tell you that you have to do one thing over another. Your parents, friends, and family will probably be available to help weigh in on difficult decisions, but you don't have to answer to them or listen to them, either. You are the only person you answer to now.

While knowing that you are in charge can be empowering, it can be equally intimidating. I know how weird this change can feel. After a few years out of college, I attended law school and graduated, but along the way, I realized that practicing law wasn't for me. Fast-forward to the summer after law-school graduation, when I was supposed to be studying for the bar exam (that stressful exam that all law-school graduates have to pass to legally begin practicing law).

Instead, I found myself rethinking my entire future. Sure, I'd been offered a job with a prestigious law firm in D.C., but did I *really* want to go that route? After all, I had started a business in law school, and it was beginning to take off. Maybe I should focus 100 percent of my time on building this company I had created. I was so confused about what I should do.

I called my parents. I called my friends. I hashed it out with my boyfriend so many times. Should I even take the bar, if I wasn't planning to practice law forever? Everyone listened to the pros and cons, but no one had the answer. The decision was up to me—and that was a stressful realization! After several restless nights, I finally decided what I had to do. Gathering up all the courage I could muster, I just stopped studying for the bar. I swear, the clouds opened up that day and the sun came out. It really felt good to finally decide on something *I* knew was right.

From weighing whether to go to grad school or take a job, to determining how quickly you can and want to pay off those dreadful student loans, you will be faced with difficult decisions that only *you* can make. But with every choice you make, you are becoming more and more the adult you are meant to be, and a great sense of pride comes with making your way through this admittedly stressful process.

To give you a little helpful guidance, we have gathered a series of essays in this chapter from postgrads who have recently made that same journey. From fruitless job searches to graduate-school applications to taking jobs that had absolutely nothing to do with what they had studied in college, these girls have seen it all. Some found instant success; others had to try a few different things before discovering the right path for themselves.

What these young women all have in common is the resounding message that if you face those real-world challenges with a positive attitude, nothing can stop you from getting to where you are meant to be. And that makes the difficult real-world transition worth the effort in the end.

How "52 Cups of Coffee" Eased the Real-World Transition

Megan Gebhart
Michigan State University graduate

Graduation day is the first day of the rest of your life. The first step into the real world. Which means that if you don't get the perfect job—and have the perfect plan—you've set yourself up for irreversible failure.

This was the terrifying belief that consumed me during my senior year.

At the time, I assumed I would have a fancy job in a cubicle somewhere, scaling the corporate ladder one rung at a time, inching closer and closer to a promotion and an increasingly impressive job title and salary.

Because that's what people expected me to do with my expensive college degree.

And that's probably what I would be doing if I hadn't embarked on my crazy experiment in caffeine and conversation. I decided that every week for a year I would have coffee with a stranger and write about what I learned in the process. I named it "52 Cups of Coffee" and called it an experiment because I knew meeting fifty-two new people would change my life. I just didn't know how.

I never expected that it would inspire me to give up the job search, sell most of my belongings, and spend an entire year traveling to more than sixteen countries, twenty-eight states, and seventy-five cities. Essentially twelve months of waking up excited about the uncertainty of where the day would take me.

It all started during my sophomore year of college, when a stranger (to me, at least; he was actually a friend of a friend) asked me to coffee and I said yes without expecting much. I certainly didn't think that meeting would turn into a lifelong friendship. One day I was reflecting on that experience, and my curiosity got the best of me—if one small new connection like that could change my life, what would a year of new connections do?

I figured there was only one way to find out. I set up my class schedule so I was free to meet people on Wednesdays and Fridays, developed the website (52cups.tumblr.com), and wrote the introductory post to kick off the experiment. At the time, I never expected that over the course of a year, I would have coffee with such a diverse group of people, including a homeless man in my hometown, Apple cofounder Steve Wozniak, a six-year-old Native American, and the wife of the Romanian ambassador to the Netherlands.

I didn't have an exact recipe for finding people. The process was a mix of serendipity and taking chances—much like real life.

U Chic's Reality Check

College is a perfect time to start building professional relationships, and the sooner you start the better! Wondering how to start your own "52 Cups of Coffee" experience with a complete stranger?

- **Identify someone** who shares similar interests or has experience in your field of study.
- **Ask!** This step is the scariest, but with practice it gets much easier. Reach out via a phone call or email to explain who you are and why you are interested in meeting. Then ask if the person would be willing to meet for twenty minutes. The meeting will likely last longer than that, but asking for only twenty minutes shows that you respect their time.

- **Do your research.** Knowing more about the person or industry and having a few questions in mind will help you feel prepared for the meeting and ensure that you have plenty to talk about.

- **Listen!** This is the most important and often the most difficult part. You're there to learn, which won't happen if you talk the whole time.

- **Follow up.** Thank them for their time, and if the meeting went well, stay in touch—you never know where a new connection will lead you!

I reached out to people I knew of through social media or other campus and community events and asked friends and mentors for recommendations of people who might be willing to have coffee with me. My original intent was to stick to people within my community, but over time, a powerful thing started to happen—the more people I met, the more confidence I found to reach out to people I didn't know at all.

I started reaching out to notable individuals I found fascinating: a graphic artist in Chicago I admire, the inspirational female entrepreneur in Detroit I saw on the news, a world champion ultra-marathon runner competing in the same half marathon I was preparing to run in Washington, D.C.

At the same time, I started receiving unsolicited emails and tweets from people interested in connecting or friends wanting to make introductions to their fascinating friends. I had coffee with Jonathan Zittrain, a Harvard Law School professor, because he reached out to me via Twitter and it just so happened that we were attending the same conference in Austin, Texas. I met Piotr Pasik, a graduate student at Michigan State, because a good friend emailed me and insisted that I include him in the project.

I found that saying yes to unexpected opportunity (that I could pay for, thanks to my part-time job) led to tremendously interesting experiences.

Case in point: When I met Piotr for coffee, I never would have predicted that six months later I would be a guest in Piotr's childhood home in a rural town in Poland and that his 86-year-old grandmother would become Cup 40 of the project.

That was the magic of this endeavor—the constant uncertainty of what the next cup would bring. I didn't know who I would meet, what I would learn, or how I would change from each encounter.

Hearing stories from all walks of life—teachers, entrepreneurs, artists, executives, parents, athletes—has had a lasting impact on me, and a positive one at that. Seeing the world from many perspectives taught me the most important lesson I could have learned before graduating: Success isn't about having a perfect plan. Moreover, life doesn't always go according to plan.

Life throws you curveballs. Sometimes good ones—unexpectedly falling in love, discovering a passion, stumbling into an incredible career opportunity. And sometimes ones that test your strength—losing a loved one, losing your job, facing an unexpected illness or tragedy.

I heard all of these stories and more, which led me to a realization. Understanding that life won't go according to plan leaves you with two choices: let the fear of the unknown overwhelm you or embrace the uncertainty.

At the start of my senior year, I was terrified of the uncertainty that graduation would bring, but by the end of 52 Cups, I found the uncertainty exhilarating.

Why? Because over and over again, I heard stories of people navigating the uncertainty well, taking risks and finding great success and happiness despite the challenges and setbacks.

For example, Torya Blanchard, in what she calls her *Fight Club* moment, decided she was going to quit her teaching job and cash in her 401(k) to start a (now-thriving) restaurant in Detroit. Stefan Olander was happy being a Nordic ski instructor when a friend convinced him to start working for a tiny athletic company called Nike. Fifteen years later, he is the vice president of Nike Digital Sport.

> Understanding that life won't go according to plan leaves you with two choices: let the fear of the unknown overwhelm you or embrace the uncertainty.

Tom Izzo, Michigan State's head basketball coach, was so determined to become a head coach that he was willing to work as a graduate assistant for the MSU basketball team, living off a measly $4,000 salary at age 30, because that's what he had to do in order to one day become the head coach.

Every story taught me a lesson in how to react when life doesn't go according to plan and, more importantly, showed me that instead of worrying about having the perfect plan, I should focus my attention on making the most of the situation I find myself in today. Because if you can make the most of today, you'll create opportunities for tomorrow.

> If you can make the most of today, you'll create opportunities for tomorrow.

While it was scary to tap into my savings account and plan a trip while all my friends applied for impressive jobs, I knew that I was making the right choice. The stories I heard gave me faith that if I trusted my instincts, they would lead me in the right direction. Thankfully, my assumption was right. When I stopped looking for the perfect job and focused on what I loved, the perfect job found me.

After I had traveled for six months on my own, Michigan State's alumni association offered me a marketing job where I would travel to various cities to connect with young alumni—a great position for a traveler with a love for good conversation.

And what happens once that job is over? I don't know. But that's okay.

I know that if I can figure out what I love to do, find the courage to do it, and do it well, life will work out, and I'll have a lot of fun in the process.

A Journey Toward Self-Discovery

Jenna Zhu
Swarthmore College graduate

It seems like yesterday that I had just completed four grueling years of intensive study in political science and psychology. For the most part, I enjoyed my areas of study, but as I approached graduation, I found myself in the greatest period of uncertainty I had ever known.

I was jobless, possibly homeless, with a degree from a liberal arts college that was not leading to any foreseeable career prospects. I had spent the past five months applying for job after job in my field of study, doing informational interviews all over, and networking like crazy. The result? Zip. Zero. Zilch. So no surprise, I was discouraged, but I was even more angry at the pressure I felt from significant others in my life—mainly my family—to "do something with my life." Didn't they know I was trying?

After finally scoring a job interview with an organization for which I had previously interned in Washington, D.C., I decided I would strike out on my own. It was time to prove myself. Luckily, a generous alum allowed me to live with him and his wife for a month for free, as they had when I was an intern. However, what had started out as a promising venture quickly brought dismay when I learned my application for a full-time position had been rejected by the organization. That was a huge blow to my confidence, forcing me to realize and accept that I could not just rest on my laurels and qualifications to get a job in the field I thought I wanted.

Refusing to give up, I redoubled my efforts, applying for any position where I could use my skills—medical interpreting, door-to-door sales, telecommuting—and even got some offers. The more I did this, the more doors opened. Then, one day, I got called for an interview for my dream job—a staff assistant position at an international organization I deeply admired.

It was the hardest interview to prepare for, not in terms of the content, but because I wanted it so badly. The entire process seemed to be out of a dream. After what seemed to be a successful interview, I sent my follow-up materials, wrote a thank-you letter, and later learned that I was accepted. Hallelujah! Things were beginning to finally look up. The job itself was not easy by any means. In fact, I had never worked harder. At the same time, I was still dealing with my internal struggles, so it felt as if my big dreams were far from being realized.

U Chic's Reality Check

If you are having doubts about your own direction in life, try the following:

- **Journal every day, even if only about trivial matters.** Self-reflection is a cultivated habit and can help you work through these issues of uncertainty.
- **Confide in people you trust about your struggles.** Support is key to recovering (or discovering!) one's sense of self.
- **Ask yourself: Is there a lack of connection between my professional and my personal goals?** If so, how can I bring them more in line with each other?
- **Do not give up on your dreams.** If you're facing an especially trying time, know that this, too, shall pass; the darkest hour is just before the dawn.

However, the more I thought about it, the more I realized that happiness is not a state of being, but a process. "Follow your bliss," American mythologist Joseph Campbell says, which references the Sanskrit concept of "Sat-Chit-Ananda," meaning "being," "consciousness," and "bliss" or "rapture." However, all of this bliss can come only through fire, and I knew that my journey was just beginning.

I began to pour myself into self-development, entering into a period of deep meditation. Being independent allowed me to carve out a lot of quiet time for reflection, and I acknowledged a lot of the important parts of myself that I had hidden away during my time in college. I acknowledged my own deep sense of depression, how tough I had been on myself at times, and the eye-opening realization that my personal voice had been suppressed for the last twenty-one years.

> [T]he more I thought about it, the more I realized that happiness is not a state of being, but a process.... [B]liss can come only through fire, and I knew that my journey was just beginning.

Thanks to the pressure my parents had placed on me growing up, I lived my life to make them happy, studying something I did not want to, taking jobs that did not fulfill me, and denying myself of many needs, such as time for myself or small pleasures. For so long, I had been unable to just be me.

Now, I was entering into brand-new territory as a hero of a saga. I emerged from this cocoon awkward and uncomfortable. I realized my independence, not a job, was going to give me the greatest gift—self-knowledge and freedom to be myself. What matters most after college is not what job you get or even who you know but who you become.

As I moved through this period of uncertainty, I realized that I had always known the desired profession of my heart: to be an actress in film, theater, and television. I had just ignored it before in favor of making others happy. Now, I began to take classes and accept acting roles on the side. Eventually, I started to get paid to do what I love. Getting there was a tough process because there was no one who could give me directions as to how to live my new life. I realize now that this was the greatest blessing, for I finally had the freedom to figure it out *and* to do it on my own.

If you are facing some of the same ground-shifting struggles and questions after college, I would advise you not to underestimate the importance of your twenties, for they are a formative period of time. Few things in this lifetime are permanent, but your own sense of self can always be trusted and will be your most important tool for finding success in the real world.

How a Rebuttal to a Grad-School Rejection Letter Changed My Life

Jeni Hunniecutt
King College and East Tennessee State University graduate

Graduate school was my backup plan. It was my "I don't know what else to do" plan.

I had been an intern with the Social Security Administration for about a year and a half and had decided that was the job I wanted. Oh yes. Great pay, great benefits, job security. It was perfect on paper.

Unfortunately, I couldn't get that oh-so-perfect job postgraduation with my BA because the government placed a hiring freeze on noncritical federal entities. Government lingo for, "We aren't hiring." However, I held out hope, waiting for the freeze to lift so I could jump on board as a permanent government employee.

In the meantime, I thought, "Why not go to grad school while waiting? What do I have to lose?" Having the degree would be useful down the road anyway when I wanted to move up the ladder to a management role.

The school that made sense for me to attend was only forty-five minutes away. It had an MA program for communication studies, which was what I studied in my undergraduate program, and offered financial assistance to graduate students. Plus, acceptance was a sure bet.

I mean, it was only the nearby state university; everyone gets in there. So I took the GRE, wrote my statement of intent, and asked my then-professors for glorious letters of recommendation.

I didn't bother applying anywhere else because, in addition to being confident

I would get in, I wanted to stay in the area. So I applied. And waited. The waiting part wasn't bad at first. However, as it became more of a sure thing that the Social Security Administration wouldn't be able to hire me as a permanent employee after graduation, waiting for the acceptance note to arrive began to get a little more nerve-racking.

And then I got the email about a month before graduation.

Rejected.

I couldn't believe it. How had I been rejected from this sure bet? I read the email four times and then stared blankly at the screen as my heart started to beat faster and faster.

"*Dear Ms. Hunniecutt, We regret to inform you…*" I was devastated. How could I have been so stupid, so arrogant?

I slammed my pink MacBook shut and walked across the hallway to my bedroom, where my boyfriend at the time was sleeping because he worked night shifts. I crawled into bed with him and started sobbing. He heard me, woke up, and asked me what on earth was wrong.

"The school rejected me!" I explained as I wiped my eyes and hid my face in his chest.

"*What? Why?*" The surprise in his voice made me feel a little better.

U Chic's Reality Check

Planning on applying to graduate school? Here are some essential tips for you:

- **Do not underestimate the safety schools on your list**, especially these days when more folks are applying to more places, giving even those safety schools their pick of the litter. They may end up being stricter in their admissions requirements than you might think! While you may think you are a shoo-in for at least one of the schools you applied to, have a backup graduate-school plan just in case you don't get accepted to any place you applied.

- **Cross your t's and dot your i's—twice!** Stay in contact with the admissions office while you are submitting your packet, and make sure they have received all of your documents. Also, they want passionate students in the incoming class who will contribute in a positive way to the class dynamic; it can't hurt for them to get to know you as someone who *really* cares and is thorough.

- **Somewhere in your application, show why you want to go to each specific school.** (Even safety schools want to know.) Otherwise, the school could see straight through your application and reject you because they suspect you won't attend or won't contribute as much as other applicants who clearly do want to go there.

I explained what the letter said, and he tried his best to tell me it would all be okay and I would figure something out as I always do. I wasn't listening, though, because I started thinking more and more about those reasons they gave me for the rejection.

The reasons didn't make much sense, at least in my opinion.

I got up and walked back across the hallway to where my computer was sitting, taunting me. I opened it and read the email for the fifth time, rereading the reasoning behind the rejection. My letters of recommendation aren't from enough academic sources. What? I asked *three* professors to send letters. My statement of intent and described goals weren't a match for the program. Huh? I wrote them based on what a professor in the program told me the program offered! My GRE scores were low? Okay, this was the only reason that made more sense.

I waited a few hours so that I could calm down and collect myself, and then I sat back down at my MacBook and hit the "reply" button on the email. I developed an articulate and respectful argument, hitting each reason they gave me with a rebuttal. I defended my credentials; I explained why I would excel in the program; and I politely asked them to clarify some points they'd made in the rejection.

My favorite line was the last one I wrote: "I respectfully accept the decision of the board but might I also respectfully suggest that the board be more observant of applicants and consider more the wide range of factors that play into the potential success of a student in graduate school."

Wham, bam, thank you, ma'am! It felt good to send the letter, even if they didn't end up reversing the decision. Whether this letter would change their minds, whether anyone would actually see it, I didn't know, and honestly, at the time I didn't much care. It just felt so good to stand up for myself.

Wham, bam, thank you, ma'am! It felt good to send the letter, even if they didn't end up reversing the decision. Whether this letter would change their minds, whether anyone would actually see it, I didn't know, and honestly, at the time I didn't much care. It just felt so good to stand up for myself. I immediately started working on Plan B.

U Chic's Reality Check

Were you rejected by all of the schools you applied to? Have a good cry or make a long phone call home to your mom. Then it's time to move forward with a good plan:

- **You are your best advocate.** If you truly feel the rejection was a mistake or some piece of your application was missing or overlooked, it's okay to check with the admissions committee or at least ask for advice about reapplying. Many people don't get accepted to graduate school until their second or third try.

- **Sometimes, last-minute spots open up in a class for various reasons.** So check online message boards or with other programs, or both, to see if the school has any last-minute openings or someone has heard of any opportunities.

- **If you do decide to send a rebuttal letter to a rejection, take time writing it so that you develop a sound argument that impresses the readers.** Most of all, be respectful. Your response may not change their minds, but you will impress them as someone with a lot of gumption *and* class.

- **If you choose not to pursue it, take comfort (and we know that's not easy!) in the fact that things happen for a reason.** The right thing will come along in due time.

Sure enough, not even a week later, I got another email from the university. "*Ms. Hunniecutt, It is our pleasure…*" There it was. I was accepted.

My letter worked! Not only did it work, but I was commended on my ability to articulate such a valid argument and to defend my credentials. As it turned out, two of my letters of recommendation had been lost in the admissions process and never made their way to my application packet.

If I hadn't had the nerve to send the letter responding to my rejection, no one would have ever known this, and I wouldn't be where I am right now—working toward a master's degree. In addition to acceptance into the program, the school offered me a graduate assistantship, which meant *they* would be paying *me* to participate in their program. I was ecstatic!

U Chic's Reality Check

Maybe you weren't rejected by your top-choice grad schools, but now you are waitlisted. What to do? First, don't give up hope. Don't be afraid to check in with the admissions committee from time to time when you're on the waitlist. Call to inform them of important updates—such as a job promotion or a certificate you recently completed—that could affect their final decision. If you stay in touch and show that you genuinely want to be a part of their incoming class, the school may be more inclined to bump you to the top, giving you a greater chance of ultimately making it in.

Students are rejected from graduate schools all the time. And most of the time, schools reject applicants for valid reasons. However, there are special circumstances where the school makes a mistake. A friend of mine experienced a similar situation when a pharmacy school he applied to lost part of his application packet and rejected him based on inaccurate data. I urged him to call the school and dig deeper into his rejection. It worked, and he started in that program this fall.

Arguing against a school's rejection isn't going to work for everyone, but responding politely and articulately to a rejection and verifying that the reasons for the rejection are valid and make sense is something every prospective student should do—if not to make sure the school didn't make an "uh-oh," then to at least to know how she can improve her application the next time. I'm glad I stood up. Who knows what I would be doing today if I hadn't?

Craigslist: A Postcollege Love Story

Gracie Bialecki
Pomona College graduate

When I was sixteen, I fell in love. Not with a boy, but with a website. Craigslist.

It was never a place of killers, lurkers, or fiends—it was a place of opportunity, a place where you took your problems and found low-cost solutions.

The first time I used Craigslist was to buy sold-out tickets to see Bright Eyes, my absolute favorite band. I was sixteen, and the interaction involved strangers meeting up with my dad at his apartment in Chelsea. It was the best concert I'd ever been to, and through the transitive property of flawed teen logic, my obsession with Bright Eyes morphed into a deep, faithful love for Craigslist. It became the obvious alternative to homework, the first site I went on when I got home from school, and in my teenage vanity, I religiously checked the Missed Connections section to see if anyone had fallen for me from afar.

In college, Craigslist helped me furnish the garage I was living in, but I didn't have time for extensive browsing and was too busy being a student to need to search for anything like a full-time job. Still, it was the only site I'd ever used to search for jobs, and by senior year, as my classmates started getting offers and signing contracts, I begin to wonder if I should find a more legitimate means of seeking employment.

I majored in English and knew that I wanted to write. I didn't want to teach or work at a desk or be a secretary or go into marketing or go into "consulting," whatever that means, or do literally any of the jobs my friends had.

At one point, as the anxiety of my senior year of college became unmanageably soul crushing, I crawled my way into the career development office.

"What are your interests? What kind of place do you see yourself working in? What are your career goals? Where would you like to be in five years?" These were not questions I had answers to.

"I just want to know how to find a job without using Craigslist," I replied.

They sent me away with a stack of books, pamphlets, and résumé guides, all of which languished on my desk until I faced the facts, recycled them, and accepted my return to "the List" as inevitable.

After graduation, all I knew was that I wanted to live in Brooklyn, write, and somehow avoid any mind-numbing nine-to-five desk jobs. So, sitting on my parents' couch, I opened my computer, gazed at the comfortingly familiar purple font of the Craigslist homepage, and set to work.

U Chic's Reality Check

While Craigslist can be an excellent postcollege resource, don't forget to take precautions. How many scary stories have we heard in the media about creeps being up to no good on the site? Here's how to protect yourself:

- **Read carefully.** The ads people post, as well as the emails they send you, can be very indicative of their nature. Try to avoid ALL CAP ADS, ads that are grammatically incorrect, or ads that lack important information, as this can say something about the poster's state of mind.

- **Meeting strangers you've connected with on Craigslist can be nerve-racking, so always bring a friend.** It helps to assuage any fears you have and will help keep you safe.

- **Trust your instincts.** If the person is hard to communicate with, unreliable, or rude, take your business elsewhere. There are people on Craigslist who are honest, friendly, and fair business people; don't feel pressured into anything, and remember you can back out of a deal at any time.

Craigslist was there for me whenever I was adrift. Its simple, unchanging format and interface was one constant in my ever-changing, always unknown life. Jobs, apartments, the future could all be found using links on the site, or so I told my anxious self. And sure enough, instead of gaping existential questions, there were answers: a two-bedroom apartment with reasonable rent in Bushwick and a job interview for a copyediting position at an up-and-coming Brooklyn graphic design agency.

So Craigslist got me to Brooklyn. A mover (found, of course, on Craigslist) moved all the furniture from my brother's old apartment to my new place. Soon after, I acquired an Ikea bed frame via a girl on Craigslist, and an adorable kitten, Ophelia, via a family on Craigslist, to share the bed with me.

But even with all this, I still found myself at loose ends. My job at the design agency was in limbo, and though I kept looking, there were no other promising leads. My days were endless; weird expanses of time suddenly stretched before me, and I had no idea what to fill them with. I hadn't settled into a routine, hadn't starting seeing my friends regularly, hadn't figured out how to feel productive while being unemployed.

Craigslist was there for me whenever I was adrift. Its simple, unchanging format and interface was one constant in my ever-changing, always unknown life. Jobs, apartments, the future could all be found using links on the site, or so I told my anxious self.

I found myself immersed in five projects at the same time: typing two sentences of an email, working briefly on a short story, then getting up to wash dishes, while installing a doorknob in the bathroom and organizing my closet. Worst of all, instead of writing any coherent stories or making any progress I was proud of, I wasted hours, wandering lost through Craigslist.

U Chic's Reality Check

Social media can help you uncover opportunities you might not have otherwise found. But it can also be addictive and become an unnecessary distraction, if you don't keep the surfing time in check. Here's how not to become a social-media junkie:

- **Focus.** Tell yourself you are going to finish the important tasks at hand—like that email or cover letter—before you start mindlessly clicking through friends' photo albums.

- **Log out.** Instead of leaving Facebook, Twitter, and Instagram permanently open, set a number of times per day when you'll check them, and sign out after you're done.

- **Turn off the Internet!** If you have something important to write, quit your browser, turn off your AirPort, or go to a café and don't ask for the Wi-Fi password.

I decided I had to limit myself to one session of Craigslist a day, so I checked it while I drank my morning cup of tea. This stopped the hours from pouring into the limitless void of possible jobs, brief gigs, and free furniture. During one of these once-a-day sessions, I responded to an ad calling for bookworms to help critique the beta version of a literary website.

It was the easiest way I've ever earned twenty-five dollars, and despite my best efforts, I was absolutely unable to stop flirting with the kind, attractive employee who was facilitating my evaluation. Eventually I worked up the courage to email him, and we started seeing each other. I quickly learned that, although it was the honest answer, telling people we met on Craigslist elicited only confused looks and scandalized responses.

U Chic's Reality Check

As fun as spending hours on sites like Craigslist and Facebook was in college, it's time to move into the world where future employers, not just your friends, will be looking at your online profiles. Here are a few tips to keep in mind:

- **Facebook isn't going to get you a job, but LinkedIn might.** Devote your time and energy to professionally focused social-media sites that benefit your personal brand.

- **Go for a trip down memory lane and clean up your Facebook account.** Untag all those pictures of you with a red cup in one hand, and check the privacy settings to make sure future employers are only seeing what you want them to see.

- **What you say and do, especially on the Internet, may come back to haunt you.** Never complain online about your job, boss, professor, or any specific individual, as your complaint will always be there for the world to see. To prevent something you'll long regret from ever happening, pause for a moment and think about what you are posting, blogging, or tweeting before you do. Consider the result a reflection of your professional self, so take time to proofread and show the world the best version of you.

I've lived in Brooklyn for two months now, and without Craigslist, I wouldn't feel nearly as settled in as I do. Craigslist is a world where you can get what you want if you look hard enough. It is a world where people come together and help each other and share and give. And it seems honest enough to say that Craigslist has given me most everything I have today: an apartment, an adorable kitten, a bed, a caring companion, small amounts of money, and perhaps most importantly, the occasional writing gig that keeps me engaged in something I so deeply love.

A Real-World Crash Course, Eight Rows at a Time

Anna Michels
St. Olaf College graduate

Driving a tractor was not something that I thought I would ever be able to list in my skill set. Writing, editing, research, the usual trappings of a liberal arts graduate—and in my case as a Norwegian major, a strong inclination toward obscure foreign languages—sure. Tractor driving? Not so much.

But, as I perched on the hydraulic seat of a 200-horsepower John Deere tractor (my tractor, for the next eight weeks and 3,000 acres), I realized that a lot of the skills I had depended on in college were going to be useless in the cornfields of rural Illinois. It was time to shed my cap and gown, pull on a Carhartt coat, and learn to be a farmer.

Like many of my friends and classmates, I didn't have a concrete plan for what to do with myself after college. I knew that I wanted to be an editor for a book publisher, so I attended a well-known graduate certification program in publishing to get a leg up. But without any real contacts in the industry, I didn't see how I was ever going to break into that world. Soon September rolled around, the class below me headed back to school to begin their senior year, and I still didn't have any kind of job lined up.

So when a friend of a friend asked me if I was interested in driving a grain cart for the fall harvest to make a little extra money, it wasn't a tough decision.

U Chic's Reality Check

Didn't get your dream job coming out of college? Here's how to make the most out of any job you get:

- **Keep an open mind.** You never know which aspects of a new job may spark new passions or interests, or lead to meeting great new friends.
- **Learn as much as you can**. Every experience is valuable, even if it may not seem relevant to your life right now.
- **Look for ways to use the experience to eventually attain your dream job.** Regardless of how unrelated your current position may seem, there are probably aspects of it, such as organization or teamwork, that will make you a stronger candidate for the job you really want.

"Grain carting," as I soon learned to call my job, didn't require a whole lot of brainpower. Basically I was responsible for following the combine around the field and collecting the grain from its relatively small holding tank. I would then race back across the field to dump the corn or soybeans into a semitruck, which would take the load to the dryer or the grain elevator. At our busiest times, we had three semis running at once, and I was hauling loads of corn weighing upward of 50,000 pounds. Working around so much heavy machinery was nerve-racking at first, but I soon settled into the monotonous grind of twelve- to sixteen-hour days performing the same repetitive tasks over and over again. After less than a week, I began to get bored.

There isn't much to do inside the cab of a tractor, even a fancy one with a radio and an air conditioner like mine. We didn't break for lunch and worked straight through the day, eating our meals out of coolers that we kept in our cabs. I listened to a lot of Top 40 radio, gritting my teeth through songs by Ke$ha and Flo Rida but unwilling to settle for the alternative, sitting in silence. I was living by myself and working such long hours that I was too exhausted to do anything in the evening besides heat up a can of soup, struggle halfheartedly with my extremely slow Internet and collapse into bed.

Even though it was tedious work and I occasionally felt isolated, there were aspects that I actually liked—like getting time to write more. One day, along with my dried mango and pretzels, I packed a small notebook and pen into my tote. Rather than staring glumly at my steering wheel during the numerous three- or four-minute breaks I got throughout the day, I started writing a story. Two or three sentences at a time, with one eye on the combine to make sure that it didn't get too full, I scribbled frantically in my notebook. Amazingly, the hours started to pass more quickly.

By the end of the season, our little harvest crew had become a strange family of sorts: seven middle-aged to elderly men, who ate "dinner" instead of lunch and drove pickup trucks with built-in toolboxes—and me.

At the same time, the men driving the semis, who had initially patronized me, began to trust me not to run my tractor into their rigs, and we would chat briefly as I handed over my paperwork for them to take to the elevator. Brian, who drove the combine, was my constant companion over the CB radio as we circled the fields together, churning through 3,000 acres of corn eight rows at a time. I took a lot of flak from the guys for being a girl, and Jack, who was old enough to be my grandfather, got a huge kick out of violently pounding on my door to wake me up if he caught me napping in my cab.

By the end of the season, our little harvest crew had become a strange family of sorts: seven middle-aged to elderly men, who ate "dinner" instead of lunch and drove pickup trucks with built-in toolboxes—and me.

If you had told me during the first week of the harvest that I would end up loving my job driving the grain cart, I would have thought you were crazy. But soon, the little things—a notebook in my cooler, a few jokes with Brian over the CB, spotting a deer bounding out of the cornfield—made the boredom worth it. I discovered that, even after the parties and excitement

U Chic's Reality Check

Have to learn something new for a job, something you never expected or wanted to learn? Here's how to pick it up quickly and efficiently:

- **Don't be embarrassed to admit that you don't know something.** Your supervisor will likely expect you to have questions, so go ahead and ask.
- **Double-check your work until you become comfortable.** Go over each step in your head and think it through carefully, rather than acting on instinct simply to get it done more quickly.
- **Learn from your mistakes.** You *will* make mistakes—and that's okay! Learn from them and move on without being too hard on yourself.

of college, all it really took to make me happy day after day were a couple of friends and a few small distractions to break up the long hours of work.

As September turned into October and the afternoons shortened, one of the farmers' wives would often pack an entire dinner into the back of a pickup truck and drive it out to the field for us. I would climb down from my tractor, knees creaking and stiff from sitting in the same position all day, and grab a plate of fried chicken, biscuits, and mashed potatoes. Sometimes it was a big slow cooker full of chili or boxes of pizza and garlic bread. The food didn't really matter, as long as it

Standing among the broken shafts of cornstalks and holding my plate under my chin was a far cry from the college dining hall, just as driving a tractor was a far cry from churning out a dozen papers a semester. But each experience was satisfying, and no matter the work—hauling grain or writing theses—I found a way to enjoy it every day.

was hot and there was plenty of it. We chowed down, grabbing fistfuls of napkins to sop up the grease and dropping crusts and chicken bones on the ground.

Standing among the broken shafts of cornstalks and holding my plate under my chin was a far cry from the college dining hall, just as driving a tractor was a far cry from churning out a dozen papers a semester. But each experience was satisfying, and no matter the work—hauling grain or writing theses—I found a way to enjoy it every day. At the end of the harvest, I was actually sad to lock the door to my tractor for the last time.

These days, tractors are just something I absently notice as I drive to work. After a few months of an unpaid internship, I landed my dream job as an editorial assistant at a book publisher—a job that challenges me every day. Even though I'm not working on a farm anymore, some things remain the same. I still wear my Carhartt. I still carry a notebook with me wherever I go, and I try to take a few minutes throughout my day to relax, chat with coworkers, and decompress. I still work a lot—and probably will for most of my adult life—but I know now that work and play aren't mutually exclusive. And that's not something that you'll learn in any classroom lecture.

U Chic's Real-World Essentials—Real World Bound

- **College is a perfect time to starting building professional relationships to help ease the transition into the real world.** The sooner you start, the better! Identify someone who shares similar interests or has experience in your field of study. And then? Ask them to have a conversation about it! This step is the scariest, but with practice it gets much easier. After all, the worst they can do is say no.

- **Having doubts about the direction your life is taking?** Take a step back and ask yourself: Is there a lack of connection between my professional and my personal goals? If so, work on trying to bring them more in line with each other. If not, do not give up on your dreams. If you're facing an especially trying time, know that the darkest hour is just before the dawn.

- **Social media can help you uncover opportunities you might not have otherwise found coming out of college.** But they can also be addictive and an unnecessary distraction, if you don't keep the surfing time in check. Instead of leaving Facebook, Twitter, and Instagram permanently open, log out. Set a number of times per day when you'll check them, and sign out after you're done.

- **Didn't get your dream job coming out of college?** Look for ways to get the experience to eventually attain it. Regardless of how unrelated your current position may seem, there are probably aspects of it, such as organization or teamwork, that will make you a stronger candidate for the job you really want.

- **Accept that you will make mistakes in life.** Nobody is perfect, and that's okay! Learn from them and move on without being too hard on yourself.

Looking for more great advice? Head to www.UChic.com/Diploma-Diaries, where you will find our favorite resources and websites—they come highly recommended by our guide's contributors and editors. Be sure to leave your suggestions as well!

CHAPTER 2

Where to Live?

Where to live? Good question. This is one of the first big decisions you'll face on your way out of college. After all, this is the first time you really get to choose where you want to be, and that decision can influence where you end up in life—in terms of both career and lifestyle.

For a variety of reasons, some of you may be moving back to live with your parents, or you may already be living with them. Not having to pay rent or utility bills for the time being can be a relief, but of course, this is not an ideal situation. When you're trying to be an adult, it doesn't help when childhood rules start to rear their ugly heads again. Curfew, anyone? For some of you, this option might be mortifying, especially if you're the only one of your group of friends who doesn't have your own place.

On the other hand, some of you might be facing the decision of whether to stay in the college town you have come to know and love over the last several years or to pack up and move all of your belongings to a new town, where you're lucky if you know anyone.

When I was graduating from college, I chose to stay in my college town of Lawrence, Kansas, to finish up the few credit hours I had left toward getting second degree in French. Sure, I didn't have near-term plans to live and work in France, but why not? Not only was I getting a second degree, but I'd still be seeing some of the same faces on a campus where I'd thrived. Heck, I could still be involved in some of the activities on campus that had been such a blast to participate in during my four years in college.

I was wrong. A key detail I neglected to consider was the fact that others didn't necessarily have the same plans. Many of my closest friends moved to other states right after graduation, including my boyfriend. No one told me how different things would be once my closest friends weren't around any longer.

Suddenly, I felt really out of the loop, not sure if my presence in certain activities and clubs made sense anymore. I was so much older than the other members. (Well, only by a year or two, but I felt old!) Long story short, it was a lonely semester, so much so that I eventually decided I needed a new adventure, choosing to join my boyfriend, now husband, in Philadelphia where he had just started graduate school. It was a decision that, while scary at the time, I am glad I made.

In this chapter's essays, you'll see a variety of takes on the question of where to live. While reading them, you may discover a connection to something you are experiencing. Or you may not. Either way, what you will find are some of the same emotions you are likely to feel as you sort out your own living situation after graduation, so take comfort in the fact that you are not alone.

Not My First-Choice City, But I Made It Work Anyway

Vanessa Thurman
Ohio State University graduate

I hate moving and always have.

It's exhausting. I hate throwing things out, and I get really attached to "the way things are" once I've settled them a certain way. I don't even like to rearrange furniture.

So, after college, the shock of having to join the real world didn't make me as uneasy as the possibility that I might have to move. That really scared me. I was having none of it and spent several hours every day searching for a job within a twenty-mile radius of my apartment.

I was living in Columbus, Ohio, and loved it. My friends were there; the cost of living was low; and with 50,000 students sharing a campus at The Ohio State University just down the street, the city had a young, eclectic vibe that seemed impossible to beat. Columbus felt like the perfect size—large enough that I still hadn't explored every sight there was to see, but small enough that I started regularly running into friends everywhere I went. I loved running into friends. I felt like I was a part of a community.

Unfortunately, a few months out of college, the dream job literally down the street still hadn't revealed itself. I had even expanded the search. The next town over wouldn't be so bad, right? Throughout all of this, I was turning down jobs across the country because I didn't believe I could be happy anywhere else.

I held out as long as I could, being absurdly picky and watching my savings slowly dwindle. Finally, one day the stars aligned and the job offer of my dreams fell into my lap. I'm not kidding—it was perfect. I couldn't say no anymore.

The catch? I would have to move to Madison, Wisconsin, some 600 miles away.

There's exactly one reason that I didn't chicken out and miss this amazing opportunity. In a fit of determination, I said to my friends and family: "Don't let me change my mind. The second we get there, I'm going to want to turn around. But I have to take this job—it's the right choice."

They took me at my word, thankfully. And so, a few weeks later, I found myself being held hostage in the back of a SUV. My parents and I sat in downtown Madison while I tried to decide which one of the apartments that we'd seen was the least depressing. I was in tears and furious with them for not letting me back out of my word.

My life would be terrible here. I would be buried in snow for months, lonely and bored. It wasn't worth it, I reasoned.

U Chic's Reality Check

Didn't end up in your dream city? Here's how to make it work:

- **Find out what makes your current location special and explore it.** Maybe it wasn't *your* first choice, but more than likely, there are people around you who really love where they live. Find out why!

- **Get a map.** Anytime you move, you open up a whole new set of options for day trips and road trips. Did your relocation put you hours closer to the beach, the mountains, or the birthplace of your favorite artist or musician? Plan some weekend adventures!

- **Make friends and stay social.** You can easily do this by joining clubs and organizations related to your personal or career interests. Or consider taking a class on a subject you've long been interested in but never had the time to pursue, like photography or painting. Anywhere you live, you're going to like being there a lot more if you're surrounded by people who share similar likes and interests.

This probably doesn't come as a shock, but I was completely overreacting.

In the beginning, being in Madison was daunting—I really didn't know a soul in the entire state. And I'm not the bubbly type who strikes up conversations with everyone I meet. But, believe me, after a few days of sitting silently in your apartment, you'll talk to people. You'll talk to the grocery-store clerk, your boss's kids, the parking-lot attendant…anyone.

After a little while, it became kind of fun, though. I made a point of striking up conversations with my neighbors, my coworkers, and the girl who made my coffee. I waved to people I saw when I was out jogging or buying bread. It was important at first just to talk to people to feel like I still existed. Over time, when I ran into them later in a yoga class or at a party, some of those people became friends. And then close friends. And I felt that sense of community around me again.

I made a point of striking up conversations with my neighbors, my coworkers, and the girl who made my coffee.…It was important at first just to talk to people to feel like I still existed. Over time, when I ran into them later in a yoga class or at a party, some of those people became friends. And then close friends. And I felt that sense of community around me again.

After Madison started to feel like home, my parents said something that really surprised me. They commended me on my ability to adapt and make the best of pretty much anything. "Apparently," they said, "we can just leave you anywhere. In a week, you're organizing indoor soccer leagues and planning barbecues."

Me? Really? I had never thought about myself that way.

But they were right. I'm never going to love boxing up my stuff, saying good-bye to friends, or being the new kid—it really does suck. But moving to Madison turned out to be a great experience. I had made new friends, re-established movie night, and found the best (veggie) burger in the city. I even met my husband, although I didn't know it at the time. Before long, I had recreated the happy life I had in Columbus. In time, Madison also became a place that I loved. The snowstorms there are, indeed, pretty terrible. But otherwise, it's a great place.

U Chic's Reality Check

Still fantasizing about living in that dream city one day? Don't give up hope. Here are some ways to stay on track toward eventually ending up where you want to be:

- **Budget wisely.** Put aside money from every paycheck for your "moving fund." Nothing takes away options faster than being broke.
- **Network.** Meet as many people as you can and talk about your goals often. Join professional networks that will connect you with people in your industry who can help you find work in other cities. It happens more often than you might think.
- **Just go!** If living in your dream city is the most important thing to you, pick a date, save your money, and come up with a plan. You might have to wait tables for a few months while you find your feet, but the only thing that's really stopping you is yourself.

What if I had found a job inside that twenty-mile radius of my college town and never left? Would the world seem as large and available to me as it does now? Would I have ever realized what I was capable of? I'm grateful I didn't give myself a chance to find out. There's too much to miss out on by staying put.

On Moving Back Home... with My Parents

Ashley Cobb
Ball State University graduate

As graduation approached, I pretty much assumed that life would carry on once I left college.

Unfortunately, there weren't many writing jobs in central Indiana at that time other than writing for a newspaper, and most marketing and public relations positions required more experience than I had at graduation. With no job prospects on the horizon, I packed up my stuff in my tiny off-campus apartment, said good-bye to Muncie, Indiana, and continued my journey as a young adult with a big move...right back into my parents' house. Definitely *not* where you want to be at the age of twenty-two, if you know what I mean.

Moving back into the house of my teen years brought back many memories. Many good and some I had hoped to forget: having to abide by the 10 p.m. curfew my parents had set because "Nothing good ever happens after ten," according to my dad; sneaking out with my best friend to a party where, of course, there was underage drinking; and the inevitable embarrassment of puking all over my dad's shoes when I returned home after one of those illicit nights out during high school.

Moving back into the house of my teen years brought back many memories. Many good and some I had hoped to forget.

At first, moving back in with the folks was tough. I was used to living on my own and being in a college town where anything goes. My parents decided to set a certain number of rules that I had to follow to live in the house. I had to find a job, regardless of whether it was my dream job or not; I couldn't drink in the house; and I had to call to let them know if I was going to be out late. I got a job as a retail manager, and looking back, those rules weren't particularly hard to follow, just different from what an independent college graduate was used to.

During college, I had emerged from my shell to become a social butterfly, so I wasn't really fond of leaving a party early just to get home on time for the folks. In fact, that became a major sticking point with the move home. While they expected their little girl (I swear they still look at me as if I'm an eight-year-old!) to be home around 11 p.m., I had a different idea for a curfew, especially if I wasn't working the next day.

Many a time, I tried (unsuccessfully) to quietly open the door around 3 a.m., only to hear Dad grumble as he came down the stairs in his undies, "Where were you? We were worried sick! You could've just called your mother to let us know you were going to be out so late!"

During these moments, I felt like I'd just gotten caught stealing cookies from the cookie jar, having to apologize profusely. The result? An awkward silence between my parents and me for the next two days. And trust me, living in the same space as your parents as a young adult is tough already, but doing it with the silent treatment is not fun.

This scenario continued for more than two years, as I couldn't find a job that would financially support my living on my own.

U Chic's Reality Check

Facing a big move back home to live with the 'rents? Understandably, this may be the last thing on earth you want to do postcollege, but as we all know, sometimes it's unavoidable. Here's how to make it work:

- **Talk with your parents and establish common ground on what is expected on both sides.** Moving back home after college is an extreme change, so be sure that your parents and you are both on the same page.

- **Don't be a complete mooch.** Sure, your parents raised you with lots of love and affection, but they don't necessarily want to have to take care of *all* your needs now that you're an official adult. Besides, you won't feel good, either, when they do things for you that you should be doing for yourself. Offer to cook meals for the family or be willing to serve as a tutor to a younger sibling who might be struggling in school. By doing your fair share, not only will you and your parents enjoy the experience more, but you'll develop a mutual sense of respect that will go miles toward easing any tensions that may arise.

- **If you don't have a job, get one, even if it's an unpaid internship or a managerial position at a restaurant or your favorite retail store.** You'll feel more productive and gain experience you can refer to during your next job interview, and working is way better than sulking at home.

- **Try to get out of the house as much as possible.** Of course, you'll want to spend time with your friends, but also look for local networking groups where you can meet other young professionals in similar careers or industries who may know of opportunities for you. And who knows? You may even end up bumping into your future employer!

I continued to hang out with a few of my college friends that lived in the area. Several guy friends had rented a house just north of Indianapolis that was also close to a neighborhood bar that we frequented. Every night after work, we would head over to the bar to play pool, have several drinks (we became best friends with the bartender, Bubba), and then head back to our friends' house, where insanity would ensue.

One night, a new guy showed up with one of my friends. Evidently, he'd just started working with my friend and had just moved to Indy from Hawaii. (Why anyone would do that, I have no clue.) He was tall, had tattoos along his biceps and calf muscles, and had a great smile. He was just the kind of "bad boy" I loved. Well, it turned out that the bad boy and I got along *really* well. He and I would bond during the wee hours of the morning as he told me about never meeting his dad and how his mom kicked him out of the house at fifteen and now had nothing to do with him. These sad tales went on and on.

As we grew closer, he manipulated me into spending about $3,000 to $5,000 within three months (although I didn't see it at the time), thanks to my decent-paying job that allowed me to go out on occasion. And then it got worse. I missed my period.

I remember the exact day, time, and place where we were when I told him. We were both in shock. We had only had sex once, but I was stupid and hadn't demanded he use a condom, nor was I on birth control. His face turned red as we both began crying together. What would we do? My religious background had taught me that if it ever happened, God forbid, we *had* to get married.

Thankfully, my parents felt otherwise. Although they had been strict with me growing up, they didn't want me to go down the wrong road. My father and I had a tough talk when I shared the news I was pregnant. My parents had always disliked my bad boy, but when I told my dad that I was getting married because it was the right thing to do, it was like a light turned on in his head and he realized what we, as a family, must do. He knew the man was manipulative, played games, and cheated. My father didn't tell him that he couldn't be my child's father, but Dad insisted that there was no way in hell we should get married.

> When I look back, I wouldn't change a thing. While I now live on my own, having to live with my parents postcollege taught me so much—most importantly, how to be a great parent.

Then I had my son. It was the best day of my life. After twenty hours of labor, lots of puking, and an emergency C-section, my favorite little man arrived. My son was perfect, with blond hair and blue eyes. And yes, the "bad boy" was there, although he isn't in the picture now.

My parents, whom I had resented for so long, were there as my son and I lived in their house for two more years, and their supportive presence during that time cannot be replaced. My son, now eight years old, looks to them as his second parents. They helped me through the nights of continuous screaming, his first walk into my arms, and the first time he said, "Papa."

When I look back, I wouldn't change a thing. While I now live on my own, having to live with my parents postcollege taught me so much—most importantly, how to be a great parent.

Being a "Grown-Up" in a College Town

Sara Aisenberg
University of North Texas graduate

I often say that I feel years older than my friends.

We're all about the same age—in our early twenties—and we've all graduated from college. Most of us are in a committed relationship, and we also all have jobs of some sort.

So why do I feel so much older than my friends who, essentially, are in the same boat as I am?

Well, here's the thing. I graduated a semester early. I started working full time immediately after graduation. I moved out of my parents' house and joined my long-term boyfriend in our own apartment across the country. If this doesn't add up to being an adult, then I don't know what does.

The funny thing is that although I'm an adult, according to all definitions, I find myself living in a college town—Columbia, Missouri. (Mizzou-rah, anyone?) This has presented some challenges to fully embracing the adult life.

So far, things are working out, but being a grown-up can be tough—especially being a grown-up in a college town of approximately 110,438 people.

A typical day in my life includes some version of the following: getting up and getting ready for work, kissing my boyfriend good-bye, working from nine to five, going home, cooking dinner, taking the dog for a walk, and hanging out with my boyfriend in the evening. I also manage to work in blogging, watching TV, reading, cleaning the apartment, or some combination of them all. The list would make my mom proud.

Sure, there's the occasional fun of a happy hour or dinner gathering with friends, but these activities are few and far between.

Being in a college town, I find myself stuck in the middle of a place where college students are still partying hard while adults, like myself, are trying to hold steady jobs. I find it hard having to explain to my college friends why I can't stay out at a bar until 1 a.m. on a Tuesday, no matter how much I want to enjoy the college bar specials.

Being in a college town, I find myself stuck in the middle of a place where college students are still partying hard while adults, like myself, are trying to hold steady jobs. I find it hard having to explain to my college friends why I can't stay out at a bar until 1 a.m. on a Tuesday, no matter how much I want to enjoy the college bar specials.

On the other hand, Columbia is home to many young families, and that presents some interesting challenges as well. At my boyfriend's recent company picnic, for example, we were one of the only unmarried couples there. On top of that, we were the only guests without kids, which was totally weird in a different way. Of course, everyone who works with my boyfriend knows that we're not married and don't have kids of our own yet, but we still felt a little out of place because we weren't chasing after our kids in the pool, waiting in line for face painting, and talking to other parents about school.

Now, I don't feel pressured in any way to grow up faster because of these differences. It's just that they make for an awkward existence during an already awkward time in one's life—that stage of quasi-adulthood right after college.

But what makes this existence really tricky is that I look like a college student, and in a college town, that means I get treated like a college student. This isn't always bad—when I can take advantage of student discounts without having to flash the student ID that I may or may not have held onto, for example. For the most part, however, I'd prefer a little more respect, having earned my stripes as a hard-working adult.

U Chic's Reality Check

As an adult living among a sea of students in a college town, do the following to help establish yourself as a hard-working grad:

- **Dress the part.** As comfy as it is to wear Nike shorts and college T-shirts day in and day out, make an effort to dress decently for work and when you're out and about around town. There's a time and a place for sweats and flip-flops, and in postcollege life, it's mostly at home. It's amazing how differently adults treat you when you look like one of them, rather than like a student who just rolled out of bed to go to class.

- **Be confident in what you have accomplished and be a resource for others.** If you run into someone from your college days and they ask what you're up to, let them know where you work and how much you love your job. You're a college grad who has a great life, so be proud of it! People will be impressed by what you've achieved. On the same note, reach out to your student connections if your company is looking for an intern. They'll be grateful for the opportunity.

- **Enjoy your free time, get involved, and give back.** Your community has been good to you and helped you get where you are, so why not give back to it or to other organizations? There's plenty of stuff to do in your little college town, so take advantage of it!

Sometimes, I think I should wear a sign that explains my situation: that I'm a twenty-two-year-old college graduate; that I have a full-time job with health benefits; and, that while I live with my boyfriend, we aren't quite ready for marriage. And kids? That won't be happening any time soon, if we have anything to say about it.

When I think about it, it's a little bizarre that my normal routine involves going to work, doing grocery shopping, paying my bills, and then going to the bar with friends later in the day. But at this point in my life and in the town I live in, this *is* my normal and I'm making the most of it.

Sure, I'm not thrilled that my apartment complex is once again filled with hard-partying students, now that summer is over and school is back in session. But on the other hand, I love the cheap cost of living, and I can't wait for football season to roll around so I can enjoy some good, old-fashioned tailgating.

U Chic's Reality Check

As an adult living in a college town, you may feel like a fish out of water. After all, you now have real-world responsibilities, but you're surrounded by students not much younger than you who want you to come out and party like you used to on Thursday nights. Here's how to make the most of it:

- **Hang on to your student ID.** You'll be amazed at the great discounts it will get you (movie theaters, restaurants, bars, stores and services, the campus bookstore, and so on.) Nobody needs to know that you're *technically* not a student anymore.

- **Do the things you loved to do as a student.** If you attended every football game, buy season tickets (or tickets to the games you want to attend) and continue to cheer on your team. A lot of schools offer student prices for season tickets for at least a year or two after you graduate, so take advantage of the discounted price. If tailgating is more your scene, get a group of friends or family together and tailgate just like you did during college. Then head to a bar or to someone's apartment to watch the game. It's the perfect mix of college and adult fun!

- **And while you're enjoying those college perks you still have access to, it is also okay to set new "adult" limits on the entertainment**, like earlier bedtimes and maybe a little less craziness on those nights out with the girls. After all, you definitely don't want your boss catching you doing something stupid!

- **Enjoy the inexpensive cost of living that a college town can offer.** You'd probably pay a lot more for the same apartment, groceries, utilities, gas, events, and drinks in a bigger city.

Honestly, when I step back and think about it, living in a college town isn't all that bad. Maybe I should be thankful that I'm learning how to be an adult in a place that caters to individuals who are still in school and on their way to adulthood. It helps make this complicated transition a little bit easier.

Columbia has been good to me so far, but since I won't live here forever, I'm excited to see what comes next.

New Kid in Town

Kara Apel
University of South Carolina graduate

When I was finishing up my job search, I had two job offers in two very different cities.

At first, it seemed like a no-brainer. Since I'm from Ohio, I thought I would love to be closer to home by taking a position about four hours away. After going to school in South Carolina (about eight hours away from home), I was sick of being on my own.

But somehow, this opportunity in Augusta, Georgia, seemed way too good to pass up. So I went with my gut and was Augusta-bound in no time—even though I had only been to Augusta once (for my job interview) and didn't know *anyone* there.

There was a lot to adjust to at first. I wasn't able to find a roommate, so I was living on my own. That was hard in itself because I'd never lived without a roommate—ever. I didn't quite realize how scary it would be until my first night alone.

Once I got over that, my first Friday night alone proved to be even scarier. Who in the heck would I hang out with?

Before the big move, I didn't consider who I

> Before the big move, I didn't consider who I would be hanging out with in this new city.... I had too many other things on my mind at the time! But right after graduation and right before the move, I suddenly realized I didn't have anyone to call, even if I wanted to do something.

would be hanging out with in this new city—it's something I didn't really think much about in the chaotic run up to college graduation. I had too many other things on my mind at the time! But right after graduation and right before the move, I suddenly realized I didn't have anyone to call, even if I wanted to do something. It was an incredibly scary feeling, one that I'm sure every young professional in a new city goes through at some point.

After spending that first Friday night bored, twiddling my thumbs, I realized I needed to make a change. I needed to make friends, and to do that, I would need to put myself out there.

U Chic's Reality Check

Making new friends in a new town after graduation can be tough. Here are some tips to help you break the ice:

- **When someone invites you somewhere, always try to say yes.** If you keep turning people down, they will stop inviting you places.

- **Don't be afraid to be the first to invite someone to hang out.** Who knows? They might be just as interested as you are in making a new friend but might be too shy to ask.

- **Be open to new experiences and opportunities.** You never know where you will make new friends or who they might be. You'll also be surprised at what you might bond over!

- **Just be yourself.** Don't try to be someone you're not—putting on a façade is too tiring, and it creates unsustainable expectations in your new relationships.

With all the advice thrown at you about how to nail that job interview and how to succeed in the "real world," nobody ever tells you how to make friends once you're out of college.

Looking back, making friends in college is much easier. You've got a bunch of people your age living in the same environment as you with similar interests. I realize now just how much I took my sorority for granted—that was a great way to make friends on campus! It was nice being able to walk into the house for lunch and dinner and be surrounded with friends, something you won't really find anywhere outside of a sorority.

I was lucky enough to have joined a workplace with many other young professionals who, like me, were living in a place away from friends and family. Everyone was very friendly, but for the first couple weeks, it was hard.

Whenever I'm trying to get to know new people, I always feel the need to be my "best self." I feel pressure to look good, put extra effort into my hair in the morning, and be especially bubbly at all times because I'm worried that no one will like me if I don't. That's what was hard about it all. Even when I was out and about with my coworkers, it felt more like a chore than a fun time because I put so much pressure on myself to be perceived a certain way.

Because of this, I burned myself out fairly quickly. After less than a month of living in Augusta, I started turning down invitations to dinner or get-togethers. I didn't like feeling out of my comfort zone and having to try so hard. That's when I started using my friends who lived in nearby cities as a crutch. I would make weekend visits just to get out and see some familiar faces. Instead of staying in town and trying to make it work, I was being a coward and running away from the unknown.

U Chic's Reality Check

Some of the first friends you will likely end up making in your new city are your coworkers. Here are some tips on how to start those friendships with ease:

- **Ask a coworker to go to lunch or coffee with you.** Try to avoid talking about work so you really get to know each other.

- **Try not to gossip too much with your new work buddies.** The workplace can be a lot like high school, with gossip spreading like wildfire. Don't be the one who gets caught spreading rumors—that is definitely a reputation to avoid at work.

- **Have a work event you're obligated to go to? Ask a coworker if he or she would like to carpool and attend together.** You'll also feel less awkward since you won't be going to the event solo.

- **Bond with colleagues over similar interests.** Do you both have dogs? Ask your coworker if he or she would like to join you at the dog park sometime. Do both of you love to run? See if he or she would like to train for an upcoming 5K with you. It's a great way to connect with someone while also getting to know your new town.

A conversation with a coworker made me realize my cowardice. We were having a typical Monday morning conversation, telling stories about the weekend, when I told her I had been out of town.

Sometimes, you just need a wing woman (or two) to make you feel more at ease. Once I found some close friends in my new city, I knew everything would be all right.

"You're always out of town," she stated flatly.

She wasn't trying to be hurtful with this statement; it was true. I was always out of town, so when I got invited anywhere over the weekend, I would turn the invitation down. If you keep turning people down, after a while they will stop inviting you, which is exactly what had happened to me.

So I sucked up my fears and forced myself to stay in town. But even though I was trying to go out and be more social, I still hadn't found a close friend, someone that I completely trusted. So it was still a little hard to feel at home in Augusta.

Then, I had a stroke of luck. Two new girls started at the TV station where I worked about two months after I did, and we hit it off. I felt less pressure to fit in with them because they were new, too, and weren't sure where they fit in, either.

With these girls, I didn't feel the need to be anyone other than my true self. When that happened, I let my guard down and became closer with the people around me as well. This is when I really started to enjoy my postgrad life! Everything began to click.

Sometimes, you just need a wing woman (or two) to make you feel more at ease. Once I found some close friends in my new city, I knew everything would be all right. We had each other to navigate the weirdness of living in a new city and starting our first jobs out of college.

Living with the Boys

Kristin Nielsen
University of Nebraska–Kearney and Bellevue University graduate

My senior year of college, I lived with two of my sorority sisters in an old house off campus. It was such a fun experience that I didn't think anything could ever compare. But when our lease was up and I alone had made the decision to stay in town for the summer following graduation, I had to find a new place to live.

I had dreams of moving into my first one-bedroom apartment. I was excited about the solitude, eager to buy my own furniture and to spend the summer reading, as well as working and connecting with friends before we all moved on to the real world. I would have my own place, and I could keep it as clean, quiet, and peaceful as I wanted—something I hadn't necessarily been able to do in shared apartments during my college days.

But after a lot of searching, I found that apartments that offered the flexible month-to-month lease I needed were hard to come by. At the end of the day, it became clear that a solo apartment wasn't going to be a reality for me.

I knew I had to find another group of roommates to live with. After talking to what seemed like everyone in the town of 25,000, there was only one option: to take the unfinished basement in a house with three guys who were members of the fraternity next door to my sorority. Could this option be any worse? My mind was filled with thoughts of kegs, dirty party houses, and women doing the "walk of shame" out of the house in the morning. No thanks!

U Chic's Reality Check

Here are the qualities to look for when hunting for roommates of either sex.

- **Ensure they aren't drama-oriented.** Do they talk about friends behind their backs often? If so, they may not always have *your* back.

- **Have they had roommate problems in the past?** If they are known for moving from place to place because they have "bad luck with roommates," the problem may actually be them.

- **Are they able to set clear boundaries before moving in with regards to who pays bills, which spaces are shared and private, and how often everyone will have guests over?** If not, there may be some uncomfortable conversations after you move in. Avoid those talks by working through these potential issues *before* you decide to move in together.

What about the solitude and peaceful, clean environment I had imagined for myself?

With just over one month left in my last semester and no other option at hand, I took the dive into a true dive and moved into that unfinished basement with the boys. I tried to convince myself that it had an "industrial, contemporary feel," but no matter how hard I tried to spin it, my new home was a cold cement basement. Oh well. I hung sheets as room dividers, bought a few area rugs, put up some art, and called it "good enough."

In addition to a number of small issues with the space, there was one major problem. When I pulled back the shower curtain in the bathroom, I was horrified. The tub was black! The whole tub was *black*. I sighed. I would have to add that to my growing list of "rainy-day" projects to clean during the summer.

So back to my new roommates. These guys were your typical small-town fraternity types. They all fancied themselves to be ladies' men, occasionally had way too much to drink, and could spend an entire Saturday watching the hunting and outdoors channel while having burping and farting contests. As you can imagine, it was not exactly a dream come true for a lady like myself.

Despite our differences, I soon found that, surprisingly, these men were anything but typical. In fact, they were the most inclusive, most thoughtful, and sweetest group of roommates I had ever lived with.

Despite our differences, I soon found that, surprisingly, these men were anything but typical. In fact, they were the most inclusive, most thoughtful, and sweetest group of roommates I had ever lived with. After I moved in, they made it clear that I was "their girl" and that they would always be there for me. It was if I had acquired three big brothers. I had experienced this type of loyalty with my sorority sisters, of course, but never in such a real, unassuming, and sincere way. They changed my name from Kristin to K-Fab, and I became part of their family.

I'd thought that I would civilize them that summer, teaching them to be a little cleaner, helping them with girl problems, and making sure they were up on time for work. Of course there was some of that, but in reality, they were the ones who civilized me! They taught me what real loyalty was and how to be there for a friend, no matter what.

U Chic's Reality Check

Getting ready to live with guys? Sometimes they can be easier to live with than the gals. Here's how to make it work:

- **Be direct!** Guy roommates are great at listening to suggestions without taking them as insults, so don't beat around the bush if you have something to say.

- **When guys clean or create a project around the house, they see it as a huge accomplishment, not just a part of daily life.** Give them major praise, and they may do it again!

- **Men sometimes don't take hints as well as women, so don't be passive-aggressive.** If you don't want his shoes by the door, just moving them to his room every day won't ever make him do it on his own. He will just think you're a really helpful gal. You'll need to tell male roommates exactly what you want, if you ever want it done.

Need proof? Here's a little tale for you. I spent the day after my twenty-second birthday in bed, trying to recover after a night out on the town. All of my roommates had left and gone to work when I was awoken by the tornado sirens. The town that we lived in had random siren testing all of the time, especially in the summer, so I rolled back over and continued to sleep.

However, I couldn't sleep because the boys had left the television on in the living room. I was getting up to turn it off when I heard, "This is a severe weather emergency for Buffalo County and surrounding areas." As anyone who lives in Tornado Alley would do, I immediately went outside with my camera to check out the situation. It was, in fact, a severe weather emergency. A huge funnel cloud loomed overhead, and as I snapped a few pictures, I saw it turn into a tornado.

I ran downstairs to the basement closet, put a blanket over my head, and listened to the television still blasting in the other room. My phone was out of batteries, so I waited and listened to the weather reporter until the power went out. After that, all I could hear was the hail and the howling winds. The winds died down and I walked up the stairs, thinking about my car that had been parked outside and hoping that there wasn't too much damage. When I stepped onto the front porch, all of the other neighbors were outside as well, and we all looked at each other in shock. Light poles were bent in half and trees were in the middle of the road, but everyone was unharmed.

A few minutes later, I was still outside discussing the events with the neighbors when an SUV pulled up and stopped in the middle of the street. Two of my roommates got out and ran up to me and gave me a hug.

"Are you okay?" one of them asked. "We were calling you like crazy and you didn't answer! We were so worried about you!"

They'd left work as soon as the storm subsided to make sure that "their girl," their K-Fab, was unharmed. While the storm was raging, I was thinking about whether my car was damaged, when the power would come back on so I could shower, and other selfish thoughts. They were thinking about me! They insisted that I get in the car with them so they could drive around town to make sure that all of our friends were okay.

As we looked at the damage and the people standing outside homes that were nearly destroyed, I knew how lucky I was to have true friends like Matt, Blake, and Clint. I laughed as I reflected on how much I'd thought I could teach them, because I realized that they taught me one of life's most important lessons: It doesn't matter how stylish, clean, and peaceful your home is if it isn't full of love. The home we shared was full of more love than I ever could have imagined, and I am so thankful that my initial plans for my own quiet, peaceful apartment fell apart.

U Chic's Real-World Essentials—Where to Live?

- **Didn't end up in your dream city after college? Make friends and stay social.** You can easily do this by joining clubs and organizations related to your personal or career interests, or by taking a class on a subject that interests you but that you've never had the time to pursue. No matter where you live, you're going to like being there a lot more if you're surrounded by people who share similar likes and interests.

- **Still fantasizing about living in that dream city one day?** Just go! If living in a particular place is the most important thing to you, pick a date, save your money for the move, and come up with a plan. You might have to wait tables for a few months while you find your footing, but the only thing that's really stopping you is yourself.

- **Facing a big move back home to live with the 'rents?** Talk with your parents *before* you move and establish common ground on what is expected on both sides. Moving from college to back home is an extreme change, so be sure that both your parents and you are on the same page.

- **Still living in a college town after college graduation? Dress the part.** As comfy as it is to wear Nike shorts and college T-shirts day in and day out, make an effort to dress decently for work and when you're out and about around town. It's amazing how differently adults treat you when you look like one of them, rather than like a student who just rolled out of bed to go to class.

- **Making new friends in a new town after graduation can be tough.** Don't be afraid to be the first to invite someone to hang out. Who knows? They might be just as interested as you are in making a new friend but might be too shy to ask!

Looking for more great advice? Head to www.UChic.com/Diploma-Diaries, where you will find our favorite resources and websites—they come highly recommended by our guide's contributors and editors. Be sure to leave your suggestions as well!

CHAPTER 3

First Job Success

Did you find your dream job coming out of college? Or maybe a job that's nowhere close to it, but at least it's something? Or perhaps you took an unpaid internship guaranteed to bring that crucial "work" experience.

Or maybe you haven't found anything promising. Yet.

No matter where you are on the career path—whether hunting for a job or already climbing the corporate ladder—your career is still probably one of the foremost things on your mind right now.

You really can't help it, right? Coming out of college or even several years into the real world, everyone wants to know, "What are you up to?" or "What are you doing next?" Having an answer—*any* answer—feels way better than saying, "I don't know," or "I'm still working on it."

And this doesn't even consider how *you* personally feel about what you are doing. In my quest to display a sense of work ethic after college and after my move to the unfamiliar "big city" of Philadelphia, I decided to take a temp job at a local law firm, working as a secretary to the firm's top dog. I had about six months before I was to head to France to complete a study-abroad program for which I'd received a scholarship.

Despite the embarrassing title I held, I thought, "This isn't so bad," going into it. After all, I was eventually planning to go to law school, so what better way to get my feet wet than to work in that setting while making a little money on the side? Right?

Wrong.

No matter how hard I tried to see the bright side of the situation, it was awful. Everyone at the firm treated me as if I didn't have a brain or anything higher than a high-school diploma. Instead of being interested in putting my killer ability to research and write to use, they were mostly concerned with how fast I could type or dictate a letter. Jeez. Luckily, I got an A in my junior-high typing class, I thought sarcastically.

I can't tell you how many times I surfed the Web during work, hoping that some editorial position might pop at *The Philadelphia Inquirer.* It never did, forcing me to suck it up and stick with my original plan of working at the firm before heading abroad.

But I didn't just do my job. In the smallest ways, I still kept trying to prove that I could do more than just file things correctly—like providing my boss with additional research that I had done on my own time for an important case. These efforts eventually paid off. After a few months on the job, my boss was getting more confident about my contributions and had learned that my big-picture plan was to go to law school one day.

He started giving me juicier work assignments, and by the last month I was there, I was essentially working as his paralegal, who also happened to type fast. In fact, the best compliment I ever received from him was on my last day. "If only I had realized that you were smart sooner than I did," he said as I was packing up the few photos I had on my desk. That compliment made my day, so much so that I've never forgotten it.

From this experience, I can confidently say that no matter how imperfect your first job might be, things do get better. This is only a temporary phase you're in. Stay focused on the big picture—what you eventually want to be doing—and don't let the short-term crap (excuse the language, but there isn't a better word to describe these moments!) pull you down. In fact, with a positive attitude and the right outlook, you may get more valuable career experience than you expected.

And one last bit of advice that still serves me well: put on your blinders.

A mentor told me that long ago, and it has stuck with me. Here's how it works: Sometimes, it is easy to get distracted by what others are doing, job offers friends are getting and you're not, or naysayers who question what you are doing with your life or your career path, even though you're completely happy with your situation.

Don't let these things distract you from your goals. If you are putting your best self out there every day and know in your gut you are doing the right thing, stay the course no matter how many distractions are thrown in your path. By learning this now, you will be prepared to handle any complication that comes along.

Because this is such a hot postcollege topic, we have rounded up a collection of insightful essays that run the gamut of possible career advice. From finding a mentor to coping with a less-than-stellar first job to having to face the "waiting game" (that dreadful time when you're waiting to secure a position in your company), this chapter has you covered.

Persistence Paid Off

Erica Strauss
Kent State University and
Franklin University graduate

Everybody knows the search for the "dream" job begins well before you graduate from college.

If we're being unabashedly honest here, my search for the dream job began when I was in fifth grade. I had always known I wanted to be a writer. At the ripe old age of eleven, I pitched an article to the then-associate editor of *Girls' Life* that later ended up in print. You can only imagine what this did to my 11-year-old head!

That being said, I feel like I've spent my entire life working on landing the hot job in journalism. The desire was ingrained in me, a part of my genetics I could never deny. Everything I did, said—heck, even thought—was somehow moving me toward my future, one that was filled with endless evenings puttering away over a keyboard, spilling my soul (and probably my glass of red wine) onto the pages of whatever I was writing.

I know not everyone is so lucky to have an inherent sense of what they want to be "when they grow up." But I'm going to go out on a limb and assume that if you're reading an essay with a title like this, you have at least an inkling of the company you'd ideally like to take a paycheck home from after graduation.

But it's not my style to lie, so I'm going to be brutally frank. Brace yourself, girlfriend.

Right now, the dream of finding the perfect job fresh out of school is pretty much just that: a dream.

While even five years ago a postgrad might have been able to land an entry-level position with a major corporation relatively easily, today's postgrads aren't so lucky. Instead, many of us are flying home to shack up with our 'rents to save money, juggling internships and part-time jobs, or enrolling in expensive grad programs just to pass time (and accessorize our résumés) before the next big opportunity opens up, and we can finally jump right in, stilettos first (assuming we can afford them on the meager salary from our part-time gig at the Dollar Shack).

That's why it's so important that you do more than just get your diploma in college and that you actively pursue activities related to your career interests afterward. Landing that dream job will take elbow grease.

That's why it's so important that you do more than just get your diploma in college and that you actively pursue activities related to your career interests afterward. Landing that dream job will take elbow grease. While that lovely (and expensive) piece of paper obviously shows potential employers that you're reliable, consistent, and probably able to bong two beers at once, a diploma doesn't do much to differentiate you from the droves of other students graduating right along with you.

U Chic's Reality Check

So, what can do you to ensure you stand out like the shining star you are? Whether you're in college or the real world, begin to typify yourself. Sign up for clubs. Take on positions of leadership (mostly to prove to yourself that you can do it, but also to set yourself apart). Devote yourself to a cause. Do something that shows your commitment to your planet and yourself. Not only does that stuff look great on résumés, but it also makes you feel great. (And in the end, feeling good is just as important as looking good!)

As a chronic overachiever, I did just that: I wrote my face off in college. I was a staff writer for my campus's women's issues magazine and became its editor my senior year. And that wasn't all: I also blogged regularly for several websites, honing my editorial skills and simultaneously sharing my point of view with the world.

By the time my final semester of senior year rolled around, my résumé was padded and I felt like I was good as gold in the job department. I was so über-confident that I began applying for full-time jobs and internships three months before I graduated in May 2010. I had a head full of dreams of a corner office in a capacious skyscraper and, of course, a totally awesome benefits package. And an entire closet full of designer handbags.

Unfortunately, after giving myself a doctor-confirmed case of thumb tendonitis and a case of what I swear was carpal tunnel (although the tests say otherwise) writing about eighty custom-crafted cover letters, I only heard back from two companies—both offering me internships, not jobs, for the summer. One was completely unpaid, while the other, at a hot national mag, paid a small monthly stipend. Sadly enough, the meager pay wasn't enough to live above poverty level in the major city where the magazine was located, so with no semblance of savings and no rich relatives who could support me, I reluctantly and dejectedly turned it down.

That was it. I was a real college grad with a polished résumé, but I was living in my parent's nauseatingly drab former guest room (doilies and all).

After a good cry and several pints of Ben & Jerry's, I decided I had to put down the spoon and attack this job beast from a new angle.

So what did I do? Finding a full-time job *became* my full-time job. I got ferocious. I wasn't entirely sure why I'd only received two callbacks before, but I was going to do whatever I could to ensure that my cell phone was ringing off the hook this time around.

I started by cleaning up my online presence. Even though a lot of the jobs and internships I was applying for were more "progressive" than the norm, I knew the higher-ups at even the most liberal corporations probably wouldn't find my photos from anything-but-clothes parties my freshman year nearly as amusing as I did.

After the Internet was devoid of my extension-wearing, Edward-40-Hands-playing photos, I decided that if I was ever going to make it out of my parents' house, I had to make my own cash—no matter where it came from. So, I shifted my focus from applying for only writing and editing jobs to any job that didn't involve wearing a visor—although I wasn't necessarily ruling that out, either.

I started by cleaning up my online presence. Even though a lot of the jobs and internships I was applying for were more "progressive" than the norm, I knew the higher-ups at even the most liberal corporations probably wouldn't find my photos from anything-but-clothes parties my freshman year nearly as amusing as I did.

I landed several odd interviews in a smattering of fields and eventually picked one: entering numbers into a painfully slow content-management system for a major international retailer three days a week. While the work was almost as boring as my back-to-back sociology and psychology lectures in undergrad, the moolah allowed me to feel somewhat more independent and less like a loser whose nightstand was covered with doilies.

That summer, and a few months thereafter, I spent all of my free time searching and applying for the jobs I really wanted. I probably spent thirty hours a week applying for jobs and sent out more than a hundred more cover letters. That's not an exaggeration. I definitely made sacrifices during that unsure time. As much as I hated to do it, I waved a solemn buh-bye to my postgrad social life (which, let's be real, wasn't so hot while living in my parent's dingy guest room anyway) and said hello to my new BFFs—Craigslist, Monster.com, and Indeed.com.

I didn't stop at those tried-and-truebies, either. I also became really good friends with Google and put my J-school skills to the test by uncovering contact information for HR people at companies I admired. (Had LinkedIn been more popular in those days, I probably would have stuck with that, but y'know. Live and learn!)

Thanks to my endless Craigslist hunt, I was also able to find a few gigs that were off the beaten path but still perfect for defining *my* path. I sucked it up and began to work for free in my field to keep myself fresh. I worked with a local freelance PR guy, helping him to contact magazine editors and secure clients spreads within the fancy pages of must-read glossies. I started my own blog to keep my writing skills above par. And I blogged for other websites, too, just to get my name out there.

Around that time, I signed up for Elance.com (a website where freelancers can find gigs) and took a slew of totally underpaid yet strangely gratifying writing gigs, such as drafting press releases and fashion blogging. Granted, I rarely broke even because these jobs normally paid less than the two lattes I inevitably had to consume to get the assignments done. But the experience? That's what mattered.

Working myself to the bone writing and number-crunching (something I hated!) kept me motivated to forge ahead in my chosen field, ensuring that I would one day break free of the data-entry monster and get paid good money to do what I loved. So, I persevered. I made the time to do it all, even if it left me sleep deprived and cranky.

It wasn't until November of that year—after I had left the world of number crunchers and was instead working as a "front-desk goddess" at a local (and popular) yoga studio, practically resigned to living a life of minimum wage if it meant I got free yoga classes—that I finally got my first metaphorical bite: an email from a trusting website editor that would change everything.

Naturally, the job was one I found randomly on Craigslist during one of my maddened midnight searches. It was a celebrity-entertainment, remote-reporter position, and although I had zero experience writing about Tinseltown, I did have quite a thirst for pop culture.

I had my first interview with the editor—who was totally chill and sweet and obviously believed in me—and bit my lip in fear for two weeks afterward. Just to ensure that I didn't let this one slip away, I did all the right things: I followed up with a nice email and even sent a thank-you card for taking the time to talk to me about my obsession with the Biebs. (I'm only half kidding.)

About three weeks later, the editor offered me the job—full time and working from home (score!)—and I began my life in the paid writing field. And thus, a celebrity stalker, and *real* writer, was born.

While I no longer have that first (amazing) editorial job, I stayed with the company nearly two years before making a break. I only decided to set sail on my own after I realized that I couldn't possibly come up with another fun way to describe Kim Kardashian. ("Voluptuous vixen," "curvy socialite," "fab fashionista"—they were all so played out.)

Luckily, I had been collecting several clients on the side during my stint and realized that I had a penchant for making people care about more than Kim Kardashian's crumbling marriage (although, let's just say I was pretty darn good at that, too). I threw myself full time into creating my own freelance copywriting business. Now, I devote my time to writing for women entrepreneurs with businesses based on their passions—and making the world a better place. (I still stalk Kimmy K every once in a while, though.)

Although it's been a long and often frustrating road to where I am today, I can genuinely say that every ounce of effort I put into landing the "hot job" was worth it.

But if there is one thing I could go back and tell my former self—and this is the biggest thing I've learned from all this—it would be: Find a freakin' mentor! I went about my job search all alone, and while things worked out in the end (as they always do, am I right?), I could have sped up the process tenfold if I had given up a little bit of control and *asked for help.*

Whether you work with your university's career center or reach out to someone you admire through email, finding someone to support you in your journey is key. Getting advice from the people who came before you and who are where you want to be is the easiest and most effective way to get to where *you* want to go.

In fact, you are probably on the right track by reading this. Looking for a glimpse of what's to come? Well, the best I can tell you is this: while your pursuit of the hot job you want won't be exactly the same as mine (and I hope won't be filled with nearly as many unanswered cover letters), you have to step up to the job-search plate prepared to face rejection with grace and work your butt off toward your goals.

And in most cases, you may end up somewhere totally different but equally as good as what you envisioned.

Why the Workplace Still Feels Like High School

Jacqueline Loundy
St. John's University graduate

I always thought the next step in my life would get me away from the immature gossipers I loathed in high school and college, but they seem to be everywhere. Even in the workplace! Conversations have moved from recounting last night's crazy party in college to the corporate holiday party after graduation, but the same people seem to be brought up in both. Instead of discussing all of the details in Finance 101 via text messages, hiding the phones behind our books (so smart, our professors *never* knew), now we send emails, pretending like we are working hard to come up with the next big thing for the company.

When I first started out in corporate America, I was like the new kid in school, learning the ropes and getting funny looks from the older, more seasoned kids. I was nervous, had no idea what to wear, got lost on the first day (even though I made a dry run the day before), and above all else, spilled coffee on my new white shirt! Fortunately, I got through everything I had been anxious about on the first day.

Now, two years after graduating from college, I've realized moving into the workforce wasn't the big jump in maturity I was expecting and the stereotypes we grew up with still exist.

U Chic's Reality Check

Don't we all wish we could have known certain things before walking into a new stage of life? Here is what you need to know before starting your first job:

- **Procrastination does not pay off.** Don't keep pushing off that project you've been staring at for the last six months. Impress your boss by being two steps ahead. Besides, you don't want to get pulled into an emergency meeting where you're asked to present your work at the last minute, so try to always be prepared.

- **Don't be nervous about admitting your faults or lack of knowledge on a particular subject.** Be willing to learn from and lean on your colleagues' strengths when needed, and show them your appreciation. People like being acknowledged and valued.

- **Layoffs do happen.** Take a deep breath and don't let the threat of layoffs distract you from your work. After all, the only control you have over the layoff scenario is the control you have over the quality of your job performance. Why not give your boss every reason to keep you around?

The drama queens, jocks, cool kids, and nerds are still in us, and we all run the risk of revealing them or being pigeonholed as such. As a woman in corporate America, I know it's important to bring my best to the office every day. If for one minute I show an extreme emotion, I could be labeled as emotional. Of course, we all have moments when we have a breakdown, but there are a time and a place for everything (definitely not in a conference room full of peers).

After twenty-two years of school, I am happy to say that I don't need to pull all-nighters studying for a midterm or final. There are no more ten-page papers, and I no longer run to the mailbox two weeks after school looking for a not-so-great report card. Finals have been replaced with financial reports; papers now explain business strategies or the never-ending paperwork needed for new hires; and instead of a letter grade, my performance is graded and rewarded through an annual bonus. It no longer pays to cram the night before or my bank account doesn't feel any love!

I was able to make it through high school and college without getting involved in the chatter, so corporate America isn't any different. I control my future: there is always another report to run, a lunch date with a great friend to grab, or the ability to walk away from a negative setting.

The major difference between school and the workplace is your perception of it and the perception others have of you. In school, we always were told not to care what other people thought. However, the attitude I give off at work affects how people view me, how well I perform my work, and my ability to grow. Getting a promotion will be hard if my team doesn't support me. And I won't be taken seriously in the boardroom if I am constantly spreading rumors about the person sitting at the head of the table.

All of the group projects in college taught me the importance of teamwork, as I would not have made it this far without the help of my peers. Leaning on the people around you is important, not a weakness but a strong point to leverage the strengths of others.

U Chic's Reality Check

When starting your first job, realize that there will be stressful days. Here's how to deal with them in a positive way:

- **Often, what matters most to your superiors is how you handle a stressful situation, so you definitely don't want lose your cool.** Before reacting, walk away, regroup, and think about how you want to respond. This will save you the added stress and heartache that come from an unwise response.

- **Put your mistakes in perspective. In the scope of your career, you're going make many—it's the only way you're going to learn—so get used to that.** Give yourself a free pass, but be sure to grow and learn from it. Your blood pressure will thank you.

- **At the end of a long stressful day, it's time to detox.** You need it. Go to your favorite kickboxing class, catch up with friends over happy-hour drinks, or simply take a long bubble bath. It will get you refreshed and ready for the next day.

It's also important to keep up with and fit into the company culture. For instance, I may not watch tonight's game to be able to discuss it tomorrow, but I'll try to listen to the highlights on my way into the office. I have found that simply knowing who won the game allows me to stay active in the social conversations at my office. I would like to think my knowledge of baseball, football, and basketball has grown tenfold, but I think my sports-savvy coworkers would laugh at that idea. Although sports may not be my passion, having some sports knowledge is important in relating to my peers, and going the extra mile to know the latest gives me more credibility as part of the team.

I wish someone had told me two years ago that advancement is 80 percent drive, hard work, and ambition and 20 percent others' perception of what I am able to accomplish. I wish I knew how not to sweat the small stuff, but it's impossible to foresee what lies ahead.

I wish someone had told me two years ago that advancement is 80 percent drive, hard work, and ambition and 20 percent others' perception of what I am able to accomplish. I wish I knew how not to sweat the small stuff, but it's impossible to foresee what lies ahead.

Every day, regardless of the circumstances, I find value in walking into work with a smile on my face, because happiness truly is infectious, and I always want to be perceived as someone who works hard and enjoys the opportunities I am given.

The Waiting Game

Hannah Gettleman
University of Illinois graduate

When our parents graduated from college, a job would appear at the snap of their fingers. Or least it seems that way from what I've heard my parents say.

Most positions didn't have specific requirements beyond a bachelor's degree, and female college grads entered the workforce without hesitation if they weren't planning to get married and have kids right away.

Fast-forward a generation, and things aren't exactly the same.

I graduated in May 2012 with a bachelor's degree in journalism. I had two fantastic internships under my belt and a bunch of experience from my involvement in extracurricular activities. With these advantages in my back pocket, I shouldn't have any trouble getting a job in the industry, I thought coming out of school. Companies need people to write copy and make their websites look nice, right?

Unfortunately, I found myself jobless and living at home with my parents in the burbs of Chicago.

But instead of getting bummed out, I decided to take control of the situation the summer after I graduated. I'm a persistent person, but even I realized that my dream job was not going to land in my lap without some hard work. So I touched up my résumé and applied for a position at one of the local newspapers, sending out all of my materials. The effort paid off, garnering me an internship interview with the editor-in-chief, who saw my potential and hired me on the spot. While the job was unpaid, at least it was something!

U Chic's Reality Check

Here are some tips to help you remain optimistic during the job search:

- **If you don't get the job, ask for feedback**. Take this advice as you head into your next interview to improve your chances for the next job.
- **Reach out to former employers and ask if they are hiring or if they know anyone who is hiring.** You are more qualified to work for a former company than another candidate, based on your prior experience, and your former employers can write great reference letters for you.
- **Ask for an informational interview with a company you want to work for.** You'll learn more about what it's like to work there and also get to know other employees. Plus, when an opening comes up, you'll be prepared to apply and have that prior established relationship, which can improve your chances of getting the position.

Suddenly the summer was finished, and I was ready for that "real" job. You know, the one that offered real money and real responsibility. I checked on job postings for journalism and public relations positions almost every other day. I also took a more proactive approach by contributing stories to small websites in hopes of getting discovered.

New experiences and educational opportunities, like getting involved in a sport, starting a blog, or taking a creative-writing class enhance your skills and make you stand out among other prospective applicants. So I enrolled in a social-media class for businesses at my local community college to beef up my résumé with a skill that is of great interest to companies these days.

U Chic's Reality Check

While on the job hunt, take time to strengthen your personal brand by using social media in the following ways:

- **If you are on Twitter, don't tweet anything you wouldn't want your grandma to see.** Even if your tweets are "protected," employers have a way of viewing them, and posting something inappropriate can possibly hurt your chances of not only getting a job with the company, but of obtaining any job in that field.

- **Keep your Facebook profile clean and get rid of anything that can be interpreted as "unprofessional."** But don't close your account! Employers like to see that potential candidates have a healthy social life both off- and online. And a showing of social-media savvy might be the skill that will tip the job application process in your favor.

- **Join LinkedIn.** It may seem like another pointless social-media platform, but when you're getting started with your career (even if you don't have a real job yet), it is actually the most useful platform. In addition to including details on what you studied in college and the amazing awards you received on your profile, you can add skills and links to work portfolios, and connect with other students and professionals in your area of interest through group discussions, résumé webinars, and networking workshops. And while you're at it, connect with your former professors or mentors, or both, and ask them to make a recommendation for you.

While I remain positive about the job hunt, there's no way to sugarcoat it. Postcollege job searching sucks. In college, when I dreamed of what my life would look like in the "real world," I envisioned a great job immediately after graduation, and definitely not this little adventure I'm on.

Unfortunately, the job-hunting process has been anything but easy. I'm still waiting for someone to discover my winning résumé. I can't tell you how many times I've been asked if I've found a job or what I've been doing since I graduated. I haven't found a job quite yet, but I am still holding my head high, knowing that one day my commitment and hard work in school will pay off. In the meantime, I am taking advantage of every opportunity I have while waiting. I am certain that something will come along, and anything is better than sitting at home watching reruns of *Friends*!

First Salary Negotiations

Steph Mignon
Hawaii Pacific University and
University of West Los Angeles School of Law graduate

When my time in college was coming to a close, my excitement and apprehension overflowed in the form of a million tears. Try as I might, I couldn't stop the emotional dam from breaking when my college roommate moved out a few days after graduation. I couldn't stop the wet sobs and sniffling that made it difficult to describe to my mother what the heck was going on.

"Everyone else has grad school plans or jobs lined up," I blubbered to her as if she were there in my college apartment living room, not an ocean away. "I have nothing. No job offer. No nothing."

"You may not have a job yet, honey, but you'll find one. I promise."

Aww, the power and wisdom of moms. She was right, of course, but what I didn't realize then was how many more tears the working world would make me shed. I didn't realize that finishing college, watching roommates move on with their lives, and packing up a mishmash of Target dishes were simple challenges compared to what I'd face in the exciting world of paying my own rent, along with all the other grown-up tasks I'd soon be facing.

I landed at San Francisco International a few months later, my diploma sheathed by a piece of cardboard lodged somewhere in my suitcase between bras and underwear. I would end up renting a family property near the beach in a tiny town called Aptos, California, while hunting for a job. I'd get thirty days free but was expected to "come up" with the other half of the rental bill thereafter, as if accumulating $500 a month (my share) would be as easy as brainstorming ideas for some great party.

In the midst of a cataclysmic rainstorm that put my earlier tears to shame, I diligently formatted my half-page résumé, which consisted of an internship, a part-time job at a furniture store, and entirely too long a tenure on the Red Bull Mobile Energy Team. I also proudly listed the two writing awards I'd received, hoping that someone, somewhere, would think these made me special enough to hire.

While the West Coast beach monsoon raged outside, I sat at my grandfather's old office desk listening to the bellowing wind and browsing open jobs on Craigslist. In 2004, finding a job wasn't easy, but the search wasn't nearly as difficult as I imagine it has been for graduating seniors from the past few years. Back then, I tailored my cover letters to positions I had no business applying to. *To Whom It May Concern, I have no experience in balloon artistry and clown acrobatics, but I'm willing to learn…*

I didn't hear back from many, but I was lucky to land a few interviews, at the very least. A weight-loss center thought I'd make an excellent nutrition counselor, but I didn't think advice from a twenty-three-year-old with less than 19 percent body fat would be well received.

"Dooooon't eat THAT cookie," I pictured myself saying to an overweight housewife, while fingering a freshly baked brownie from a coworker's birthday lunch in my lap and waiting anxiously for *her* to leave so *I* could eat it. Health and fitness were important to me, but I didn't think being a weight-loss cheerleader was the right position for someone with the metabolism of a track athlete.

I had hoped that the years of experience and success my grandfather had achieved at this desk would somehow bleed into my being and carry me successfully into my future. But I was beginning to wonder if Grandpa's desk was having the opposite effect on my job search. Just then, I found a posting by a company called Brainworks. It was an advertising firm about forty miles away that helped universities come up with branding campaigns.

The job posting said they wanted a "creative coordinator," someone to help corral copywriters and designers, while handling basic office tasks like record keeping and account setup. Now *this* sounded like the job I wanted.

The Brainworks office was like stepping into an advertisement for high-end furniture and came complete with perfect lighting. Everywhere I glanced, rows of studio lights perched in the rafters above shiny, modern steel-and-black office chairs and desks. Pictures of smiling students and manicured campus lawns fanned across an enormous and very chic design table, while bespectacled graphic artists swirled them around like tea leaves, deciding the future of some great Eastern establishment's recruitment catalog. *This* was the job I was going to get. There was just one snag. I felt as confident as anyone can feel when their work experience is limited to the many colorful ways to offer someone an ice-cold can of Red Bull.

After doing my best to relay that I was responsible, eager, and an expert at Microsoft Office, Regan, the founder of Brainworks, interrupted me. "What type of salary are you looking for?" he asked me, cutting to the chase.

I stared back at him, trying desperately to hide my panic.

"Salary?" I asked, hoping to fill the awkward silence that resulted from my slow reply. I had no idea how to answer this, so instead of doing so, I quickly followed with yet another question. "What I meant to ask was what do *you* have in mind?"

"The creative coordinator's salary is $34,000 annually, plus medical and dental benefits." Regan didn't miss a beat. I'd learn later that few beats were missed in the Brainworks office. This isn't always a good thing, I've come to believe after a few more years in the working world. People who are always prepared often live that way because being in control is what's most important to them. Being in control leaves little room for vulnerability and… being human.

All that I felt in that moment, however, was utterly *thrilled* that I was even discussing salary. And $34,000! Annually! I was five seconds away from shouting, "Alleluia!" and staining Regan's face with my red lipstick. At that point, $34,000 sounded like winning the lottery. So, without thinking it through, without factoring in my rent, car insurance, cell phone, grocery bills, vet expenses for my pooch, and my shoe addiction, I said: "That sounds perfect."

TIP 1—ASK THEM

Looking back, I'm glad I passed the ball back to Regan rather than pulling some arbitrary salary amount from underneath my pencil skirt. When in doubt, always turn the tables back to your future boss.

Say, "What have you budgeted as salary for this position?" or, "What do you have in mind for an hourly rate?" It's not recommended that you don't come prepared, but this strategy can always be employed for the following reasons:

1. They know what they're willing to pay, and nine times out of ten, your future boss has done his or her own research in analyzing the company budget and the market; and
2. This can help you gauge whether or not your requirements are too high, or in the best-case scenario, too low.

Imagine this scenario: You are hoping for $34K as an annual salary, but the boss has set the position's pay at $38K. If you show your cards first, the boss will definitely use this information to his or her benefit, not yours. No boss in the history of the universe has ever said, "Well, actually I'd like to pay you *more*, entry-level college graduate. You're selling yourself short, after all. Let's make that $38K, shall we? You're worth it!"

TIP 2—KNOW YOUR BUDGET

As I mentioned, I was so overjoyed to be discussing what seemed like a healthy salary that I didn't think about whether or not the amount would meet my needs. What I *should* have done, before or during my job search, was create a spreadsheet or a list of my expenses. Some handy online software resources, like Mint.com, offer free budgeting tools. After all, you'll need to really weigh the pros and cons if you discover that what your future employer offers isn't enough for you, which leads to my next tip.

TIP 3—KNOW YOUR DREAMS

This is a more difficult for some than others. From a very early age, I always knew I wanted to write fiction. This doesn't mean that I have always been brave enough to pursue this risky career choice, but knowing what I really want to do has helped guide the career decisions I've made over the years.

U Chic's Reality Check

In many cases, the entry-level salary you've been offered won't seem like much. You'll have done your budget and may suddenly realize that what they are offering to pay you just isn't enough. You'll have to take a holistic inventory of all the factors involved.

- **Will you be learning about an industry you hope to make a career in?** Talent agencies, for example, pay their entry-level employees very little, but that doesn't stop Ivy League–educated applicants and those with grad degrees from applying.
- **Will you make contacts that will help you in the future?** I worked at an entertainment law firm as an overqualified file clerk because I knew the people I'd meet there might be instrumental in securing movie deals for the best sellers I am sure to write.
- **Can you get a second job to supplement your income?** Or do you have savings that will allow you to survive on X amount while working for less than you can afford?

- **Consider the job market.** Will the benefits from the job you've been offered provide you with something invaluable like excellent health coverage and the peace of mind of knowing that you can go horseback riding without fearing what the ER bill might look like if you don't stay on the horse for the entire ride?

When a prospective salary isn't all you've hoped for, or worse, it doesn't even meet your financial needs, do the following:

1. Look at your short- and long-term goals and how this new job might help you reach them despite the less-than-ideal pay scale;
2. Consider your savings or other sources of income to evaluate how you'll need to compensate;
3. Review the other perks of the job from which you might benefit, like health-care coverage or a short commute; and
4. Scan your other prospects: what is the likelihood that you'll be offered another better-paying job soon enough to have cash, any cash, filling up your bank account?

TIP 4—SHOW THYSELF. SHOW THEM, TOO!

Hours after my interview ended with Regan, he called to offer me the job. There was no further discussion about pay because I had already assented, with entirely too much enthusiasm.

What I wish I had said then, and what I say now when I'm negotiating my salary is this: "While $34,000 a year seems reasonable for the next ninety days, if it's okay with you, I'd like to renegotiate after I've shown you what an awesome employee I am."

I have had good luck with this strategy, but I've also been met with a stern reply that evaluations are *only* done yearly. At some companies, this is the procedure, and it's not likely that you, as an entry-level employee, will be able to change that. So before accepting anything when you've been offered a job that won't include an increase for another year, explain that you sincerely appreciate the offer but need until tomorrow to think it over. Make sure accepting the job at that salary is something that you can really afford to do.

After you've accepted the job and have been working there for close to a year, your annual review will be just around the corner. This time (and before any future job interviews…or even your first!), research salaries for similar positions online at sites like Glassdoor.com and Payscale.com. Educate yourself during the hiring process as well, but I don't recommend bringing up the information you learn in your research until you've shown the boss what you can do.

After all, entry-level employees can be huge risks for employers. They're taking a chance on potential hires with little to no experience. Thrusting Internet stats in their face before you've accepted their offer might rub them the wrong way and make them think money is more important to you than learning, fitting into their company and culture, and ultimately building a career. Sure, you have student-loan debt and a car payment, but they're trying to run a business that doesn't include entitled attitudes from entry-level employees. Save the salary comparisons for your review period, after you've demonstrated your awesomeness.

Also, remember your budget and goals from Number 3. Can you wait a year to receive a salary increase? If so, make it your mission going forward to get to work on time, follow directions, take initiative once you've learned the lay of your new work land, and prove to your boss and your coworkers that you are an integral part of the team—such an integral part of the team, in fact, that you *do* deserve a ninety-day raise and a bonus, too. I repeat, demonstrate your awesomeness.

Your first job out of college is unlikely to make you rich (though stranger things have happened, especially if you work in tech). Instead it should be viewed as a way to make ends meet, build your résumé, make contacts, and settle into the world as an adult with a new career. It's true that you've got a lot to prove as an entry-level employee, but don't let that scare you. You've done the hard work, so now is the time to prove yourself!

No Dream Job

Anonymous

In the summer of 2009, I was at the absolute top of my game. I had just finished a one-year commitment as a consultant for an international sorority, was starting a graduate program, and despite the warnings from my family and friends about the "economic crisis," I was sure that I would find a rewarding and profitable job right away.

When this didn't happen, I kept my head held high and put my bartending skills to work at the first place that would hire me. It was in a dangerous part of town and had an average of two customers at any given time, except on Thursday nights when 90-cent Busch Light brought in the classiest folks. I learned a lot working at the bar: when to call the cops on a drug deal in the parking lot and when not to, the appropriate time to switch a customer from Wild Turkey to water, and the exact force it takes for a 300-pound man to break a glass door.

While I have carried these lessons and sweet memories into my adulthood, it wasn't exactly a significant career experience. Aside from "keno guy" (keno is a gambling game that is like bingo) and a few other respectable regulars, there wasn't a soul I cared to know at the bar. Until I met Carrie.

Carrie wore T-shirts and athletic shorts with flip-flops at all times and drank white zinfandel out of a shot glass on ice. Aside from her questionable after-work attire and beverage choice, she really had it together. She was an accountant at a hotel, and every few weeks, she would suggest that I apply for a position at the front desk.

Although I'm embarrassed to admit it, deep down I felt that an entry-level customer service position was beneath me. Although bartending wasn't a glamorous job, it was a good time and I could study when it was slow (which was always). I was horrified at the idea of wearing a uniform and running into a successful classmate. A few months later, after my savings had been drained, I applied for a position at the hotel.

My worst fears were confirmed when on my first day I was asked to drive the shuttle. Thinking back to my college days, when I was so respected by my peers and so bound for success, sent shivers down my spine. The experience became "real" when, on my second day, someone asked me, "Have you always wanted to be a shuttle driver?"

Pure horror.

My worst fears were confirmed when on my first day I was asked to drive the shuttle. Thinking back to my college days, when I was so respected by my peers and so bound for success, sent shivers down my spine. The experience became "real" when, on my second day, someone asked me, "Have you always wanted to be a shuttle driver?"

Other glamorous tasks included delivering room service, vacuuming, and generally being looked down upon by certain hotel guests. To top off the embarrassment, I was totally unfit for the position of front desk agent. The computer program was beyond me, and all of my highfalutin education and experience made my current inabilities sting even more. The other agents said, "It's okay. You can just stand there."

Every morning I woke with a strange feeling that God was looking down on me saying, "Girl, today just isn't your day." My respect for front desk agents grew immensely, and I now consider it to be one of the most challenging jobs I've encountered.

A few weeks in, I met Debra. She was the hotel director of sales and a shrewd businesswoman wrapped in a Carrie Bradshaw shell, with the shoes to match. She saw something in me and offered me the position of sales coordinator, where I would help the sales managers with their events and manage the office. I was thrilled!

Little did I know that I would still be an occasional vacuum-wielding shuttle driver. However, this new experience gave me the opportunity to spend time with a lot of people that I would want to work for someday. When professionals in the area and out of state planned events at the hotel, I was often their first contact.

I wanted to walk when I realized that the hotel wasn't exactly as new, luxurious, and functional as it was advertised to be. When I left the front desk and started my job in sales, I learned that the meeting-room heat and air conditioning were barely functional, the food was subpar at best, and many of the staff that I was supposed to rely on were often absent.

Now I'll try to explain how this turned out to be a good thing.

With so many issues and problems arising with every meeting, I had the opportunity to become very close with the event and meeting planners. Because I was their point of contact on the day of their events, I was often seen as a kind of superhero—remedying problems with the wave of my hand. When the air conditioners for the top-floor meeting rooms quit (like they did every day at 3 p.m. in the summer), I brought the guests Popsicles and made them paper fans. When the cooks didn't show up or we ran out of necessary items, I became a caterer, doing whatever it took to make sure the guests were fed and happy.

U Chic's Reality Check

Didn't get your dream job coming out of college? The worst you can do is carry a negative attitude into work with you. Instead, stay positive and make the best of any experience by showing off your skills and enthusiasm. That attitude will eventually pay off.

- **What you may think is embarrassing, beneath you, or not a good use of your education will probably end up being a serious learning experience, no matter what.** Give it your all and you're bound to get something positive out of it. You'll also have an excellent story to share during that next big interview.

- **Never stop smiling, especially if you work in customer service.** You may be the only interaction a customer has with your company. If you stay at the top of your game, people will take notice. And who knows? The next person that walks in or calls you on the phone may be the company owner who will be impressed with you and willing to promote or reward you for your commitment.

- **Whether you're just starting out or already established, you still have a lot to learn.** Be open to learning from everyone around you—not just your superiors—and you'll walk away a smarter and more real-world savvy person.

I even found a use for driving the shuttle. I realized that it was a chance to have a captive audience of one—a business traveler who had no choice but to tell me about his or her line of work for ten or fifteen minutes. The trips became a series of practice interviews. I became very skilled at talking about myself—what I do and what I'm passionate about—and received multiple job offers while in the shuttle.

I'm no Mother Teresa, but I certainly had ethical issues with promising meeting planners and guests a better facility than I knew we could provide. To remedy these guilty feelings, I began

Throughout my horrifying, humbling, and sometimes hilarious experiences at the hotel, I realized that I loved hospitality. I got a high from being able to go so far above and beyond expectations that it actually shocked people, and I knew I couldn't leave that.

doing anything possible to make sure the guests I interacted with had the best possible experience. I bought blenders so our health-conscious guests could make shakes, became a personal shopper when the dry cleaning orders didn't arrive in time for a guest's big meeting, and gave away free drinks like nobody's business.

The job offers continued to roll in. You may be wondering why I didn't take any of them.

Throughout my horrifying, humbling, and sometimes hilarious experiences at the hotel, I realized that I loved hospitality. I got a high from being able to go so far above and beyond expectations that it actually shocked people, and I knew I couldn't leave that.

I did, however, eventually leave the hotel. My need for a little bit more income got the best of me and I moved on to a bigger, better position with another company. I had a lot of really great anecdotal answers during my interview. I'll be forever thankful for my embarrassing first real-world job.

Plus, I now know what my dad means when he says, "It will be a character-building experience."

From Intern to Full-Time Employee

Emily Roseman
American University graduate

After graduating from college, you might think the scariest part of leaving the comfort of your grassy quad and the bustling college lifestyle is having to move back home with Mom and Dad. On the contrary, it's confronting the unanswerable question of: Were these four years all worth it? Did all those internships matter?

After graduating from college, you might think the scariest part of leaving the comfort of your grassy quad and the bustling college lifestyle is having to move back home with Mom and Dad. On the contrary, it's confronting the unanswerable question of: Were these four years all worth it? Did all those internships matter?

You've heard it before, and so have I. With all internships, from the clerical intensive to the most honorable, "you only get out of it from what you put into it." Over the tenure of my four years as a broadcast journalism student, I learned through five rewarding internships that the way to end up on top is to exceed your supervisor's expectations.

The same goes for my daunting search for a job as a TV news producer.

Following my time as a digital editor for *USA Today* in Washington, D.C., I learned that no job comes handed to you. Whether it was cutting video to be published the next day or helping full-time staff members learn more about film editing, I tried to establish a personal credo that with every assignment or task, I would go above and beyond. I have taken that same sentiment to heart during my application process as a postgrad.

U Chic's Reality Check

The best advice when it comes to applying for jobs? Apply early and apply often. Here's how to do it.

- **Get a head start on the job-application process as early as the beginning of your senior year of college.** By having a plan in place first, you'll be able to pace yourself throughout the rest of the academic year.
- **Try to imagine asking yourself in five years, "What does my dream job look like?"** Just as you did when applying to college, use that vision to narrow down the choices to your "top ten" or "attainable" employers, and target them accordingly.
- **While applying early, stay organized.** Make a list of the important documentation each company needs, which you can easily find on their website, and start gathering these materials ASAP!

Making your first move toward full-time employment from the "for-credit" workhorse phase starts with ambition. The ability to move ahead and make the door open just the slightest crack depends on how much you want to be a part of your industry of choice.

Taking a page out of my own story, starting early on the search can't hurt, but being able to explain your *value* as an employee to a potential company is gold.

An HR manager will measure your intern skills mostly as admirable initiative rather than as practical experience. You have yet to *really* prove yourself capable, and the theoretical skills you have learned over the past four years in school will likely pale in comparison to a seasoned applicant's experience.

I've found the need to come back down to earth when working on my résumé and cover letter. It's crucial to summarize amorphous internships into a succinct storyline that can catch the attention of the hard-to-please HR executive. From providing specific software programs in which I am proficient to listing the certificates I have achieved during my college career, I attempt to separate myself from other postgrads in every application.

U Chic's Reality Check

Always the intern but never the full-time employee? Don't sweat it. Most likely, the right opportunity hasn't come along yet. Stay positive and remain focused on the goal. Also, look into ways you can up your game, such as:

- **Making minor tweaks to the way you present yourself on a résumé.** This can be an easy way to catch the eye of a busy HR executive. Consult a friend or family member who could review your résumé and make helpful suggestions. Create a polished résumé, eliminating non-essential school clubs and activities. Instead, emphasize the projects or relative work experience that would impress your target employer. To get a sense of what the company is looking for, consult their current job openings and descriptions for insights.

- **Practice making a good first impression.** Drop the "likes" and "ums" from your speech, and practice better word choice when describing your work experience in the mirror when preparing for an interview. And it never hurts to practice the interview with a friend.

- **Switch out the "club wear," sweats, and T-shirts for a more mature wardrobe.** But office wear doesn't have to mean boring black slacks and pastel blouses. Check out stores like Ann Taylor Loft or Banana Republic for clothing that is appropriate in any office environment and items you wouldn't mind wearing on your day off! If you're applying for a creative job or a position in the fashion industry, make sure your interview outfit works in accessories and accents, like a fabulous necklace or a great pair of heels, that will make you stand out.

I also focus on making lasting impressions on the folks I meet when networking. This is always guaranteed to increase my chances for those all-important one-on-one meetings with key decision makers. For instance, while covering the Republican primaries in New Hampshire this past year, I was able to make some key connections with professors and even esteemed alumni. It allowed me to get face-to-face meetings with executive producers once I moved back home and started looking for jobs in earnest.

From BBC News to the White House to England, my internships have certainly prepped me for full-time employment, but my tenacity eventually helped me secure my dream job. I am now a proud member of the ABC News Digital Media Department's editing team, and I couldn't be happier!

How I Landed My Dream Job

Pamela O'Leary
University of California Berkeley and Claremont Graduate University graduate

At the age of twenty-six, I was entrusted with the responsibility of leading a nonprofit organization, the Public Leadership Education Network (PLEN), with the mission of preparing college women to be leaders in public policy. I was able to make this career leap for three main reasons: I had found my passion early in life; I had relentlessly and daily pursued opportunities to move toward that goal; and I had a strong network supporting me along the way. I had actively built my personal brand and used it to land my dream job.

I discovered that feminism was my lifelong vocation during my sophomore year in college. College leadership experience is absolutely transferable to your postgraduation career. In my first semester as a resident assistant, two of my female residents were raped over the course of the semester. As I assisted them through their healing process, I soon learned that too many of my female friends were also survivors of sexual violence, and I was inspired to change these terrifying statistics.

Consequently, all of my campus involvement related to female empowerment. I became a certified rape-crisis counselor, cofounded a class about feminist activism, and was the student representative on a faculty academic senate committee related to tenure issues that female faculty experience. Even though my undergraduate degree of environmental science was unrelated, through extracurricular activities, I was able to realize my passion and begin gaining experience in that area.

U Chic's Reality Check

Try to discover your passion as early as possible in your twenties. Here's how:

- **If you are still in college, explore different student groups that interest you and take leadership positions.** If a group does not exist, start your own.

- **Intern or volunteer with different organizations in your community.** It's a crucial part of the process of figuring out what you like.

- **Talk to different people who work in your area of interest.** Regularly conduct informational interviews with people from diverse backgrounds.

Pursuing as many opportunities as possible has always been invaluable to my career. Furthermore, I've learned that you must be willing to take risks, not become too attached to a single opportunity you apply to, and manage rejection with a positive attitude. After graduate school, my career kept rising with an internship at the United Nations and a fellowship in Congress. Once the fellowship ended, my career momentum crashed and I was unemployed. I swallowed my pride and became a nanny. While this obviously hadn't been in the plans, I didn't let this get me down or stop me from continuing to pursue my dreams.

While baby-sitting, I gained new skills by doing volunteer grant writing for a nonprofit and working part-time at a museum. This eventually led to my being hired as a full-time development manager for the museum. Although I hated fund-raising, I took the risk because I knew that I eventually wanted to be a nonprofit executive director and needed this background. Even today, I always look for different opportunities and constantly apply to professional development programs.

U Chic's Reality Check

To land your dream job, always be looking for opportunities to flex your key strengths on things you are most passionate about:

- **Sign up for as many listservs as possible to always be informed.** Share the information you gain with others using social media. Position yourself as someone who is up to date on what's happening in your interest area.

- **Constantly gain new skills through volunteering.**

- **Have a long-term vision of what kind of position you want.**

Of all the tactics I've taken since college to get myself on the right path, the most important strategy to my success has been to create a strong network of colleagues of different ages, both peers and senior-level experts in the field. I knew about PLEN's executive director position six months before it was posted publicly because my friend from a young professional organization was a program assistant for the organization. I also had senior mentors who were connected to the organization provide strong recommendation for me. My fund-raising and political backgrounds were necessary requirements for the job, but these personal recommendations truly gave me a competitive advantage.

U Chic's Reality Check

Starting in college and beyond, always be actively building and maintaining a network. You never know who or what organization may end up being the ticket to your dream job or next big client. Here's how to do it:

- **Network with peers, direct reports, and seniors.** Don't just take from others but also support them in their career growth.

- **Be proactive in finding mentors, and constantly ask for feedback.**

- **Always deliver excellent results in whatever you do.** Build the reputation of being a hardworking team player.

And last but not least, here is the most important piece of advice I want to give you: You are the only person responsible for building your career path. The earlier in life that you discover your passion, the better able you'll be to develop more experiences that build your expertise. In addition to your main day job, always think of how you can gain new skills through volunteering. Constantly build and maintain a network that will support you through the good times and bad. Because, after all, you have also given back to them.

How My Personal Brand Opened Doors

Erica Strauss
Kent State University and
Franklin University graduate

I've always been a bit of a rebel.

Okay, strike that—I've always been a total rebel.

But while I have an inner core that's like this big-ass party for all the Lady Gagas of the world, I'm also crazy-introverted. (Books and poetry and not speaking to another human for three days? Yes, please.) Some might call me a thoughtful rule breaker, if such a thing exists.

Unfortunately, I was also always told that being a rebel was bad. Dirty. Wrong. Shameful, even.

The general consensus is that, in life, you should follow the people who have gone before you. If they're still alive and putting food on the table, then clearly they've done something right, no?

So, after you graduate from college and before you even have a chance to put that diploma on the wall (Does anybody really do that?), you should have sent out at least fifty cover letters to prospective employers, because the only choice you have after you sashay your sassy self out of your college apartment that last time is to get a job.

Preferably it will be one that requires you to anxiously spring out of bed at 7 a.m., battle traffic with hordes of caffeine-crazed lunatics, sit in a dimly lit cubicle all day, and do the same nauseatingly annoying traffic dance on the way home as you worry about what the heck you're going to eat for dinner because you haven't had time to grocery shop in two weeks. But at least you'll have benefits!

Like almost everyone else, right before I graduated college, I was well on my way on that "right track" (despite a few minor missteps). But let's be real: my inner rebel—you know, the Lady Gaga in me—was not going to just let me go the preferred route without a fight. You really think they'd let a lady in a meat dress work in a corporate office? Exactly.

Like almost everyone else, right before I graduated college, I was well on my way on that "right track" (despite a few minor missteps). But let's be real: my inner rebel—you know, the Lady Gaga in me—was not going to just let me go the preferred route without a fight. You really think they'd let a lady in a meat dress work in a corporate office? Exactly.

So, I made a conscious decision before landing my diploma that I was going to make money my way. I decided I'd do whatever it took to avoid a lifestyle that felt to me like putting the wrong shoe on the wrong foot—all awkward and stifling and totally not cute.

Luckily, that same year I came across a fairly new idea that is actually way more fun than it sounds: personal branding.

Personal branding is the concept that everything a person does, says, wears, or thinks is a representation of their own "brand." Essentially, it's the way you sell yourself to others—and it's something you're building every day whether you realize it or not.

Put another (much more fun) way, defining your personal brand is just figuring out who you are and then showing that self to the world in the best light possible. It's fun; it's challenging; it makes your life that much more pleasurable; and most notably, it never stops.

Now, two years after my fateful graduation day, I run my own successful business, writing Web copy and freelance articles for entrepreneurs and publications around the nation.

For me, someone super introverted, personal branding has been quite a liberating experience. It's become a way for me to not only figure out what my skills and quirks are and then show them off to differentiate myself, but also to prove to myself that I can do something.

But personal branding hasn't always been easy (especially since I'm not a celebrity with an image counselor and a PR strategist hanging around at all times, making sure I don't make a fool out of myself in an interview or flash my underwear on camera…but I digress).

There are two official steps to building a personal brand, if you go by the textbook. One, you have to discover your strengths. And two, you capitalize on them in any way you can. But for me, there was an unofficial step before the first step: building my confidence.

U Chic's Reality Check

To effectively build your personal brand, you'll need to add some tools to your tool belt, including:

- **A Web presence.** Register your own domain or start a portfolio with a free site like Wix.com, Squarespace.com, or Weebly.com.
- **LinkedIn.** Use this social-networking site for professionals to showcase your skills and collect recommendations from former bosses and colleagues.
- **Branded business cards, thank-you notes, and address labels.** Include all your pertinent contact information, including email address and website when appropriate. And then use them!
- **Social media and blogs. Twitter, Facebook, and your own blog are great ways to network with like-minded people and show off your expertise.** Just be sure to keep it professional.
- **Consistency.** People like to work with people they can trust. So whether that means attending that networking event every month or

returning all work-related phone calls on time, just remember that everything counts.

- **Be present!** Don't just show up online. Chat up your peers at local networking events (search Meet.com if you're unsure) and really listen to them. People love to feel important!

Since I'd known since I was a little girl that I wanted to be a writer, I wasn't hung up on the question, "Which career path do I take?" Instead, I needed to believe that I deserved the career path I wanted.

In fact, I needed to believe that I deserved anything at all.

In high school and early college, I went through some seriously damaging relationships. I'd always been a shy girl with a tendency to people-please, and unfortunately, that led me into a series of romantic trysts with men who used, abused, belittled, and hurt me in every sense of the word, and left me feeling unworthy, incomplete, and painfully lonely.

But I always had my writing. And my dream to make money doing it.

So, in going from shy girl with the crappy boyfriend to woman with her own business who gets to work in her yoga pants everyday, brand building has essentially been a lesson in character building. Building my business and my "brand" persona from the ground up has taught me things I never knew about myself. It's also shown me I'm capable of far more than I ever could have imagined while I was crying in the bathroom at 4 a.m. because my boyfriend had ditched me or hooked up with another girl while I was downstairs at his house. (Oh yeah, that actually happened.)

In my business, my personal brand and my confidence are tested every day. For example, every time I stick to a deadline, set a boundary with a client, or say "no" to more reruns of *The Real Housewives of Beverly Hills* and "yes" to another hour of yoga, my confidence, my character, and my brand strengthen.

Whether you're looking to create your own company as I have (whatever type of company that might be) or are climbing the corporate ladder with pride (and a hot pair of kitten heels), being a brand is about so much more than how others see you and whether So-and-so offers you a job. It's about owning yourself and your strengths. It's about being true to yourself and presenting the best version of you to the people you work with and who encounter you daily. And, of course, it also involves a lot of faith and following your intuition.

Still, I've made tons of mistakes in my quest to "be a brand." For a long time, I felt I had to be extroverted or seek out corporate gigs just because they sounded lucrative, even though the companies weren't in alignment with my values, or hang out at all the right networking events to build my brand. I thought there was some predetermined mold for successful people and I needed to force myself into it if I wanted to "make it." But as any girl with skinny jeans just a smidge too small knows, forcing yourself into things you shouldn't is so not fun.

U Chic's Reality Check

Whether you're a social butterfly or a wallflower, here are a few tips for making your unique personality work for you, not against you:

- **Get to know you first.** List your strengths and weaknesses. Define on paper who you are and where you thrive.

- **Seek out opportunities that are in alignment with your personality.** If you like to work in teams, for example, look for chances to do so at work or in the community.

- **Don't force it.** Don't beat yourself up if you don't like to spend half your days in meetings, or if you can't sit at a computer alone for more than twenty minutes without getting antsy. Simply acknowledge what works and what doesn't, and find ways to do more of what you're good at and less of what you're not.

Over time, I've learned that's all crap. Instead, I've created a lifestyle that feeds and fuels my unique creative spirit and builds my brand in a way that feels authentic and good to me. I've worked meditation, yoga, reading affirmations, and other introverted activities I enjoy into my workday, so I never feel burned out or unmotivated. (All right, so the excessive Frappuccino consumption probably helps with that last one.)

In turn, I've ended up landing clients who totally get me, are thrilled to work with me, and don't mind if I only want to have a client call once a week. (Best of all, they never know that I'm working in my yoga pants!) I'm excited to wake up—and be me—everyday.

> Perhaps the most important thing I've learned as a self-employed lady looking to live her brand every day is that you should never try to be anybody else. (It's called "personal" branding, not "be-like-everyone-else" branding, after all!)

Perhaps the most important thing I've learned as a self-employed lady looking to live her brand every day is that you should never try to be anybody else. (It's called "personal" branding, not "be like everyone else" branding, after all!)

One of my favorite bloggers, Danielle LaPorte, recently solidified this fact for me when she eloquently wrote on her blog, "You don't have to be fearless; you just have to be sincere."

While I'll admit a little bit of courage can go a long way in landing you the job, the man, or the life of your dreams, I think Danielle's got it right. You don't have to be anybody else to get where you want be in life. In fact, the more you stay true to yourself, the more you'll attract the right opportunities.

I'm living proof.

My Mentor Made All the Difference

Rajul Punjabi
Kean University and
Long Island University graduate

"God bless you. Honestly," a friend said to me one day as he skimmed over a literary essay I was grading. "If I were you, I'd lose my patience with these kids. This one wouldn't know what a comma was if it hit him in the face."

As an adjunct instructor of college composition, I often deal with shoddy punctuation, comical spelling mistakes (I once got an essay about the protagonist of a novel who was a hormone-raging "sex attick"), and overall lack of discipline from my feisty freshmen. But I never sweat it.

In fact, their mischievous and semi-ignorant ways annoy me to no end, driving me to give them my all as an educator. And I know exactly where I got my patience.

Flash back to seven years ago. A college senior with vivid dreams of becoming a writer (but primarily concerned with stilettos, hip-hop, and keg parties) walks into a fancy high-rise office building in midtown Manhattan. She clutches a leather-bound portfolio in her sweaty hands, anxious and excited to jump into the glamorous

I was a mess at that age, with half-baked writing skills and skewed ideas about what it meant to make a living using words. I'd watched way too much *Sex and the City* and considered myself the Indian-American version of the cute, disoriented, curly-haired career girl running around the concrete jungle—a veritable Curry Bradshaw, if you will.

world of publishing by way of a prestigious internship at one of the best literary agencies in the city.

I was a mess at that age, with half-baked writing skills and skewed ideas about what it was to make a living using words. I watched way too much *Sex and the City* and considered myself the Indian-American version of the cute, disoriented, curly-haired career girl running around the concrete jungle—a veritable Curry Bradshaw, if you will.

I stood in front of Cathy, the literary agent I worked under during the internship, with my A-line skirt, doe-eyed enthusiasm, and entirely too much nodding and yessing. I wasn't even sure what I was agreeing with her about. I was just so excited to bring Curry to life. And poor Cathy, she had to read my manuscript summaries, full of passive voice and terrible ten-dollar adverbs—a cardinal sin for any real writer. She had to explain very simple things to me that really shouldn't need explaining.

Ideally, I should have been her astute little minion. But truth be told, she would have gotten more work done if I wasn't around.

Praise the literary gods, it wasn't that way forever. In the office that spring, I drowned myself in manuscripts. I developed a much-needed reverence for the written word. There were long manuscripts and short ones and just plain sexy ones. Sometimes I wanted to pluck the words right off the page and kiss them and bear-hug them and take them on a luxurious vacation to the south of France. I wanted to love them down and buy them things I couldn't afford (I was only an unpaid intern, after all), like Chanel sunglasses and supple leather Margiela jackets.

Aside from the all-consuming affection I developed, I began to discern the type of strong writing that would make it to the public eye from the swill that made it to the "no, thank you" pile. Cathy was too gracious to ever use the word "swill" to describe writing, but I caught on. Despite my fledgling status, she gave me a voice and valued my input. She never had to tell me to get it together, but just by being around her, I knew it was time to formulate my professional identity or, as I call it now, my "hustle."

U Chic's Reality Check

On the hunt for a good mentor? It's great that you are. It's one of the best things you can do for yourself at this stage in life.

But not all mentors are created equal. The trick is to find the right mentor *for you* and to spend time developing and nurturing the relationship as you'd do with a good friend. Here's how to do it:

- **Choose a mentor who not only has the success you want but shares similar values.** Pay attention to your mentor's personal and interpersonal relationships. Are they similar to yours, or ones you'd like to foster?

- **Look to someone who has created a brand, network, and career (not just a job) for themselves.** Once the relationship is established, don't be afraid to ask how they did it. It's the only way you're going to learn!

- **On occasion, try to meet your mentor outside the office.** Find a more casual atmosphere—a restaurant or coffee shop, perhaps—to secure a more relaxed and nurturing atmosphere to discuss goals. And if you can afford it, pick up the tab. It's a nice gesture and a simple way of saying thanks for their time and support.

I never knew what a hotshot Cathy was until I observed her "hustle." While I'm rarely intimidated by anyone (it's a Scorpio thing), her giant brain made me nervous. Would I ever be able to understand writing like she does? I had to put my ego aside and observe. I learned that Cathy's business relationships are precious to her, not because she sees people as dollar signs, but because a healthy professional relationship means long-lasting success for both parties, not to mention happiness.

Cathy is not nearly as crotchety as one would expect for how hard she works. She's positive, generous, compassionate, and a bona fide badass who dispels the myth that you have to be a bitch to be successful.

Also, I was delighted to find that not all financially comfortable white people roll around in $100 bills on the floor of their penthouse apartments. Cathy has worked hard since she was a kid for what she's got and values her support system over everything. As I eavesdropped on her phone conversations more often, I began to admire her for more than her work ethic.

I hope to be like she is: a doting, affectionate daughter, aunt, and friend for the amazing people in my life.

U Chic's Reality Check

Now that the mentor has given you his or her time and attention, it's time to reciprocate by being the type of person that your mentor can be proud of.

- **Respect his or her time, schedule, and space.** Try to check in once a month if no meeting is scheduled, and definitely nothing more than that. Also, don't bother them with numerous questions that you could have figured out on your own.

- **Show your gratitude.** Flowers are nice, but so is an email or handwritten card of thanks for the guidance and support that he or she provides.

- **Show your best self.** A polished appearance, manicured nails, extra hours of work—whatever it takes to prove that you are serious about your goals and being on top of your game.

After college, as I dipped my toes in various career ponds in journalism and education, Cathy and I kept in touch. I went back and worked for her as a junior agent (I was her assistant, but she was kind enough to give me a brag-worthy title) and learned yet another yard of the ropes. It's only now that I can look back and see how much patience she had with me and how much she looked out for me as I floundered around, trying to find my professional identity.

I want my students to feel something about writing, about learning, and even about themselves. Maybe it's just my newbie status, but I was inspired so potently at that age that I'm dying to be on the other end, paying it forward in $1,000 bills.

There's something exhilarating about female camaraderie, specifically the opportunity to ride on the coattails of a woman who's "made it" yet is humble enough to never admit that she has. Knowing her provided me with a glimpse of what I could possibly achieve, and it still makes me constantly reevaluate what type of artist, mentor, and person I want to be.

Fast forward to this week, as I sift through a pile of mostly atrocious essays, coffee stains on my desk and my tank top. I write love letters to every one of the writers on their last page, starting with a compliment and then explaining where they stumbled.

Office hours are more like mini pep rallies for me. I slam my palms on the desk and yell clichéd, outdated collegiate phrases like, "You got this!" and "Midterms next week, you gotta go hard in the paint." In states of exhausted delirium I've employed many a hip-hop line, only to result in a cocked eyebrow and a "Professor P, did you just say 'That shit cray'?"

I want my students to feel something about writing, about learning, and even about themselves. Maybe it's just my newbie status, but I was inspired so potently at that age that I'm dying to be on the other end, paying it forward in $1,000 bills. The one with the patience, the blind faith, and the intellectual affection that Cathy had for me.

I recently met with Cathy to catch up and discuss our latest projects. Over prosecco and nachos, I sat wondering at what point she stopped making me nervous and started making me proud, confident, and unapologetic about my choices. I wondered at what point I began to be able to engage in real and poignant conversation about politics, relationships, and books with her.

What comforts me most is that I'm not done growing, and neither is our friendship. Mentorship evolves, molding into what we need when we need it. So whether it starts with an overzealous and clumsy intern or a student who keeps using the wrong "your," I'm ready to invest because while success is nature for some, it was nurtured for me.

Some of my female students remind me of myself at nineteen with their immaculately tacky manicures and gritty-mouthed sass. And while some genuinely don't care about their own success, I don't let that faze me.

They'll get it one day. Or maybe they won't.

All I can promise to do is restrain my eye-rolling and guide the ones with that same gleam in their eyes that I had.

U Chic's Real-World Essentials—First Job Success

- **How to ensure you stand out like the shining star you are?** Whether you're in college or the real world, begin to differentiate yourself. Sign up for clubs. Take on positions of leadership (mostly to prove to yourself that you can do it, but also because it differentiates you). Devote yourself to a cause. Do something that shows your commitment to your planet and yourself. Not only does that stuff look great on résumés, but it also makes you feel great.

- **Procrastination does not pay off in the real world.** Don't keep pushing off that project you've been staring at for the last six months. Impress your boss by being two steps ahead. Besides, you don't want to get pulled into an emergency meeting where you're asked to present your work at the last minute, so try to always be prepared.

- **Still hunting for a job, ideally one that's related to your area of study in college?** Ask for an informational interview with a company you want to work for. You'll learn more about what it's like to work there and also get to know other employers. When an opening comes up, you'll be prepared to apply and also have that prior established relationship, which can improve your chances of getting the position.

- **While you're hunting for jobs, keep your Facebook profile clean and get rid of anything that reads "unprofessional."** But don't close your account! Employers like to see that potential candidates have a healthy social life both off- and online. And a showing of social-media savvy might just be the skill that tips the job-application process in your favor.

- **A good mentor in the workplace can positively impact your career in innumerable ways.** But not all mentors are created equal. Choose a mentor who not only has the success you want but shares similar values. Pay attention to your mentor's personal and interpersonal relationships. Are they similar to yours, or ones you'd like to foster?

Looking for more great advice? Head to www.UChic.com/Diploma-Diaries, where you will find our favorite resources and websites—they come highly recommended by our guide's contributors and editors. Be sure to leave your suggestions as well!

CHAPTER 4

The Social Scene

For many reasons, the postcollege social scene is a pretty sweet step up from college. By the time you graduate, you are well-versed in how to meet new people and make new friends—essential skills for "making it" in the real world. Even better, by now, you are likely twenty-one, so no more need to stress about getting caught with a fake ID. Add to that a full-time salary, and suddenly the possibilities for fun are limitless.

Or so it seems.

Along with these advantages comes the disadvantage of not having a social network ready and waiting for you when you hit the real world, like you did when you arrived on campus. This is even more stressful for those of you who have to move to a new place where you don't know a soul.

Such was the case when I landed in Philly after college. I had just wrapped up a great four years of college, having met some really incredible people. Suddenly, I was living in a city where the only person I knew was my boyfriend, who I had just moved in with, and my fellow legal secretaries at the law firm where I was temping at the time.

Pre-Facebook, I had no way of knowing who else I might know in the city. It felt like I had landed on Mars.

For a few weeks, I'd head straight home after work, waiting for my boyfriend to arrive and for the evening fun to begin. Wrong. Besides late classes that delayed his return, he had a new group of people he was getting to know and happy hours to head off to. Of course I was invited to go along, but I always felt like the odd man (or woman) out.

After a couple of months of this unpromising routine, I slowly started getting involved in things that would help build *my own* network. With my plans to go to law school in two years, I signed up to volunteer at a local women's legal clinic. To be around people who were closer to my age, I attended lectures and events at the nearby university. I loved working out at the gym in college, so I joined a gym down the street that was known for its fantastic yoga classes.

At the very least, these activities helped me start to feel like I was connecting to *something* in my new town, and finally, I did start to meet some really great people who I could grab lunch with or meet for happy hour after work on occasion. It was by no means the same kind of fun I had in college, but it was a great start.

In the following essays, our writers provide you with the scoop on the postcollege social scene—from struggling to meet new people in a new town to finding friends in the most unusual places. The moral of these stories? Keep exploring the boundless opportunities to meet new people and grow your network. Before you know it, your social calendar will be so full that you'll need to start worrying about the opposite side of the issue—finding more balance—which, of course, is a better problem to have!

Put an End to the Work-to-Home Routine

Marissa Kameno
Quinnipiac University graduate

Getting your first full-time job can be an exciting, but for most of us, getting to work before 9 a.m. can be a shock after those late-morning wake-up times in college.

A job can be exhausting for new grads, and more often than not, you will want to cuddle up on the couch for a couple hours before slipping into bed at your new bedtime of 10 p.m. There are two certainties in that situation: You will be very well rested in the morning, and you will not have any friends.

And that's okay—for a couple of weeks.

But eventually, you'll need to break that work-to-home routine. Exploring new post-work options is likely to jump-start your social life and will make coping with your new situation easier.

A job can be exhausting for new grads, and more often than not, you will want to cuddle up on the couch for a couple hours before slipping into bed at your new bedtime of 10 p.m. There are two certainties in the situation: You will be very well rested in the morning, and you will not have any friends.

I spent my first couple of months at my new job complaining about not hitting the gym. If the problem wasn't long workdays that prevented me from spending time working out, it was the price of a gym membership, the lack of a workout buddy, a head cold, basically anything. I had a roster of excuses to use for justifying my lack of fitness.

Well, I figured out a way to kill all those birds with a single stone: CrossFit. For anyone who hasn't heard of this program, it's a grassroots fitness organization that consists of individual gyms across the country. The benefit is simple: group exercise that doesn't look more like a recital number than working out. And it will kick your ass.

U Chic's Reality Check

Tempted to hit the couch when you walk in the front door after work? Don't even go near it. Follow these quick tips to stay active:

- **Bring gym clothes with you to work and head straight to your workout afterward!** Don't even tempt yourself by stopping at home.
- **Set plans before you leave work for the day; don't leave them for after you're already settled in at home.**
- **Preset goals for yourself in regards to your new hobby or after-work activities.** This will motivate you to practice and keep up progress.

I joined with a group of my coworkers, a girl friend, and (eventually) my boyfriend, who continues to serve as consistent motivation to attend and work hard every week. We have a small office, and when the CrossFit group heads out for the afternoon's exercise, it's incredibly obvious if you don't attend (despite efforts to hide under your desk or in the break room—trust me, it doesn't work).

As for other ways to break the work-to-home routine, some of my Pinterest-loving friends took to extensive art projects and elaborate recipes. That didn't work too well for me. My artwork still mirrors my second-grade projects, and recipes with more than ten ingredients are generally too intensive (and expensive) to cook in my kitchen. Not to mention that I don't have enough dishes or counter space to accommodate my bills, let alone a full meal.

Instead, I wanted to do something new, something cool that I could be proud of. So I treated myself to my second "big-kid gift" (gifts that you can buy yourself with that brand-new paycheck). The first one was the iPhone 4, a necessary purchase for an employee of a technology company. BlackBerry owners are practically excommunicated.

The next item was a beautiful Yamaha acoustic guitar. Was I worried that I had no clue how to even strum it? Nope. I sat down with my brand-new guitar, a fresh pack of picks, and a beginner's guide to playing guitar, which I promptly ditched in favor of YouTube videos and chords on Ultimate-Guitar.com.

Almost a year later, improvement has been slow, to say the least. I still have only a handful of riffs under my belt, and the guitar sits out of tune for weeks at a time. But looking forward to coming home from work and practicing made living alone so much easier.

But what about those times when I come home after a long day of work and get cozy on my couch? Is there even a chance that the most persuasive of friends and the most appealing of plans would convince me to get up? Hmm. Likely not.

Going out means showering, picking out an outfit, doing the makeup and hair—and then I have to drive all the way across town? No, thanks. I'm quite content watching reruns of *Friends* in my sweatpants.

Instead of even allowing myself to fall victim to this situation, I try to make plans I won't want to break in advance. Making plans a day or two ahead will make it harder to ditch your friend, and the evening will seem more like an exciting night out than a chore.

And if there is nothing interesting coming up on the city events calendar, I make it easy for myself. I try not to even sit on the couch when I get home from work. Even better is when I don't look at it.

The same theory applies to filling up the weekends. Every so often, a

Saturday morning in bed is not only enjoyable but necessary after a long week. But work is more bearable when you have some time to play. I'm not saying I get up at 8 a.m. and run a 5K (well, not *every* weekend), but just relocating my weekend lounging to a park with friends or the movie theater is usually a great way to shake up my routine.

U Chic's Reality Check

If you want to start some new activities but are unsure where to start, consider the following:

- **What do other coworkers and friends do with their spare time?** Likely, you can get some options or even bond over a new shared interest.

- **What is something you've always wanted to do but never had time?** While a lack of time and resources may have restrained you in college, not any more! Now is the time to really let yourself explore by doing what you've always wanted to do.

- **Are there activities that are totally out of your comfort zone but are intriguing?** Now is the time to break habits and start fresh!

There aren't always friends to meet up with or activities to partake in. Sometimes, I end up at home after work. But that doesn't mean I automatically park myself on the couch for the evening.

If I know I'm watching *Pretty Little Liars* on Wednesday nights (let's face it, I'm not missing that show), then I use another free night to catch up on the phone with my best friends.

I also try to use my alone time to do the things I love to do. Without parents or roommates to report my whereabouts to, I have spent afternoons wandering through the mall trying not to blow my paycheck, jogging the trail behind my apartment, or sitting on my balcony reading.

The point is that there are a million things to do, even when watching TV seems to be the easiest option.

Finding Friends in the Most Unusual Places

Tracey Rector
Indiana University–Purdue University Indianapolis graduate

As I stood in the lobby of the View of the World Terrace Club in New York City on a September night in 2011, I was thinking three things:

1. Are they going to like me? 2. Is my hair a mess? 3. Was this the most insane thing I've ever done?

Little did I know that I was getting ready to make connections and friendships I will have forever. But to start this story, I have to backtrack a little bit.

For shy people like me, it's very easy to stay within your comfort zone and not explore the unknown. Growing up, I attended a very small grade school, and high school wasn't that much larger with a graduating class of around seventy. Even when I went to college on a commuter campus, the school I attended was smaller than most others. So when you mix the shyness with the small schools I attended, I really didn't have a chance to get exposed to new people or to even find others who shared similar passions and interests.

The chance for me to finally spread my wings beyond the bubble of my youth arrived the Christmas of my senior year in college. I'd asked for satellite radio for the commercial-free music, and within a week of opening the gift, I had discovered Cosmo Radio. As an avid reader of *Cosmopolitan,* I had to find out what the station was about.

The first time I listened, one of the shows was discussing something I was going through at the time, and it got me excited about the station's entire lineup. I found Cosmo Radio to be so diverse, relatable, and enjoyable that I've been hooked ever since.

College presents a plethora of new life experiences, from breakups and tiffs with friends to learning your own style and path in life. From the time I started listening to Cosmo Radio, the station has been there to guide me through all my trials and tribulations. It's strange to say a radio station has meant so much to me, but its discussions and topics have been invaluable.

Over time as Facebook and Twitter became more popular, listeners of Cosmo Radio (mostly girls but definitely some guys, too) began to connect and network with each other.

Typically when I think of the term "networking," I think of it as something I do during work or to gain contacts for later in my career. But that's not always the case. The listeners of Cosmo Radio were networking with each other purely out of our shared interest in the station and to become friends.

Typically when I think of the term "networking," I think of it as something I do during work or to gain contacts for later in my career. But that's not always the case. The listeners of Cosmo Radio were networking with each other purely out of our shared interest in the station and to become friends.

As the group grew, we knew we were more than just "listeners." Clearly this was more than just people who listened to a radio station. It was becoming a family.

We started to call ourselves the "Fake Life Family" ("FLF"), since we mostly talked online. We even gave ourselves another nickname: "Little FFFers." Yes, it's pronounced "effers," and while I'll admit it sounds weird, it actually stands for something great. "FFF" stands for Cosmo's "Fun, Fearless Female."

The Little FFFers are a diverse group of people from all different kinds of backgrounds and life experiences. It was a new set of friends for me, friendships I never anticipated making. And while we lived miles from each other, we were all close and talked about everything from beauty tips to work advice. One of the girls put it best: "If you listen to Cosmo, you have a built-in set of friends."

As everyone became better friends, we wondered about meeting up. No one was sure how many people would attend a meet-up and how we would coordinate it, but we knew we were ready to try.

One day a few people just picked the date and location. It was to be September 14–18, 2011, in New York City.

What would we call this event? After talking back and forth about it, we settled on "Cosmo Con," as it was a convention made up of listeners of Cosmo Radio.

To make planning easy, a few people started a Facebook group to share ideas and information. While nothing was ever publicized through the radio station, we just kept finding each other and communicating through social media. Eventually, closer to the event date, the station became aware of Cosmo Con and mentioned it, but the event was planned solely by listeners from all over the United States and Canada.

I sat on the idea of going to Cosmo Con for a few days in April 2011. Despite being scared of finances and meeting people I had only talked to online, I kept thinking about how incredible it would be to meet the others, as well as the radio hosts I had been listening to for years.

U Chic's Reality Check

Are you typically shy in social situations? To overcome shyness or nervousness about speaking in public or with people you aren't familiar with, you have to first believe that you can do it.

- **Remind yourself the situation is only temporary.** You aren't going to get stuck in a moment forever; it's only for specific duration of time. The bottom line: It will be over soon; you just have to pull through it.

- **Put yourself in situations that are outside your comfort zone as much as possible.** It will get easier and easier the more you do it. Ways to do it? Offer to make phone calls at work or offer to take the lead on projects. When you start to feel a little bolder, step up to volunteer for presentations. Opportunities for you to expand are out there; you just have to take the initiative, seek them out, and not be afraid to take them on.

- **Keep in mind that people don't analyze you as much as you think they do.** We all make mistakes, even the best speakers among us. If you fumble during a speech or a personal interaction gets awkward, it only lasts for that moment. Fifteen minutes after it's over, everyone has forgotten it, so you should, too!

Hence, I take you back in the lobby of the View of the World Terrace Club in New York City.

As I stood there anxiously waiting to be taken up the elevator to our exclusive cocktail hour for the Cosmo Con welcome reception, in walked the fifteen or so Little FFFers. All qualms I had just vanished. Immediately.

I walked over to them and it was all hugs. In a matter of seconds, I felt like I had known these girls for years. We took the elevator up to our cocktail party, where groups were mingling in every corner and the views were breathtaking. I would have never experienced anything like it, had I not become more involved.

That night set the tone for the rest of Cosmo Con, and frankly, our relationships with each other moving forward. It was incredible.

As I stood there anxiously waiting to be taken up the elevator to our exclusive cocktail hour for the Cosmo Con welcome reception, in walked the fifteen or so Little FFFers. All qualms I had just vanished. Immedately. I walked over to them and it was all hugs. In a matter of seconds, I felt like I had known these girls for years.

Even though Cosmo Con was only one weekend, we made the most of our time together. We shopped, talked, ate great food, toured the city—everything. We were even able to visit SiriusXM for a live broadcast of Cosmo Radio's morning show, *Wake Up with Taylor*, and then attended a cocktail party with several of the hosts the following evening. (Again, this was all planned by listeners and not by the station.)

Spending time with such incredible people showed me a new side to friendship. Not only were we "fake-life" friends, but after Cosmo Con, we became real-life friends and immediately began to plan for the next year.

There's no set topic; we talk about everything: jobs, TV, weight-loss tips, relationships, beauty advice, and more. And because at this point there are hundreds of us (with more finding our Facebook groups every day), someone has always gone through whatever you're going through.

U Chic's Reality Check

Don't be afraid to expand your friendships and relationships outside the ones you currently have. Here are tips on how to do it:

- **Remember the song, "Make new friends but keep the old—one is silver and the other gold"? It's true.** You aren't betraying your core group of friends by making new friends. It's okay to have more than one group of close friends. As the saying goes, the more the merrier. You'll appreciate each friend more, and each will help you grow as a person in unique and special ways.

- **Be more proactive about the new friends you make and keep.** Try reaching out to people who share similar interests and passions via social media or clubs you are involved in, as opposed to people you are forced to interact with because their cubicles are next to yours at work.

Nothing against your work pals, but you are likely to have more fulfilling relationships with people who share similar interests with you outside of work.

- **At every event you attend, whether for work or fun, don't be afraid to ditch the people you came with in order to meet new people.** I know it feels awkward at first, but this is really the best way to expand your network. We all know how easy it can be to get away with not having to meet anyone new because you come with a group. Also, people are less inclined to approach you when you seem to be already occupied.

All of these women I've met and continue to meet through Cosmo Radio are truly "Fun, Fearless Females," and I'm so glad to be a part of it. If there's anything I've learned from all this, it's that all women are fun, fearless females, and we can do anything.

I've also learned that you *can* make new friends outside your day-to-day life at school or work. I would never have made these friends and become a part of the "fake life" family had I not stepped out of my comfort zone and taken the plunge.

When you're in school, whether high school or college, or even in the working world, making friends is easier because you're somewhat forced to be classmates or coworkers. Sometimes, these people share the same interests as you, but sometimes they don't. It takes effort to network and make new friends that you don't see daily at school or work. For me, it was all through social media because of Cosmo Radio. It can be anything for you—all you have to do is become more involved in your interests and network, network, network!

So to answer my questions from that September night in 2011: Yes, they were going to like me; yes, my hair was a mess; and yes, it was the most insane thing I'd ever done. But it was one of the best things, too.

Keeping in Touch with Old Friends While Embracing the Next Chapter

Kara Apel
University of South Carolina graduate

Living nine hours away from my hometown is rough—there's no denying that.

I always feel like I'm missing out on everything that's going on in the lives of my friends from high school. Whether it's birthdays, a bachelorette party, or even celebrating a job promotion, I'm stuck missing out on all of it. Often, I'm so behind on the gossip and the most recent events that I feel incredibly out of the loop.

I can feel pretty lonely at times—no matter how many friends I have from college and in my new city—especially when I look through Facebook photos and see everyone together having fun.

One event that particularly pained me to miss was when a close friend gave birth to her son. I missed her baby shower and didn't get to meet her son until he was more than six months old. While I was able to get her a baby-shower gift months ahead of time, I still felt like the most terrible friend in the world. Even though there wasn't anything I could do about it, it didn't make it any easier to see pictures of this little baby boy and know that I wouldn't be meeting him soon and wouldn't get to be a part of his life. I'm not sure what's worse: the fact that I realize I'm going to miss many of these events in my friends' lives or the fact that they realize it, too.

Since I went to college about eight hours away from home, I'm used to being away from everyone. It's not a new feeling. However, unlike being in college, now that I'm in the real world, I don't get to come home nearly as often as I'd like. I especially miss that winter break when I would be home for a whole month without any worries or responsibilities. These days, since I don't have the vacation days (or the money), I can only go back two or three times a year, and I may not even get holidays off.

U Chic's Reality Check

Dealing with the homesick blues? Here's how to move past the ache to fully embrace your future:

- **Reach out to those old friends who know you best.** Arrange a time when you can have a Skype or FaceTime chat. Not only is it great to see their faces, but you can also give them a virtual tour of your new apartment. And if you can manage it, try to meet halfway. Is there a city that's roughly in between the two of you where you could arrange a girls' weekend? Book it!

- **Try to adapt to your new city and make new friends.** While they won't replace your friends from home, they'll certainly help you get over being homesick (and help you have a lot more fun).

- **Do you ultimately want to find a job in your hometown?** Come up with a career plan that will help you take the necessary steps to do just that.

- **Accept that you have to live in the present.** As much fun as the past was, you will waste valuable time by looking backward.

While my parents come down to visit me or meet me halfway for some weekends, their visits don't make up for the fact that I'm rarely within even a six-hour radius of my friends. And they're in the same boat as me—not enough vacation days or money to be able to visit me, either.

However, despite all of the obstacles, I have managed to stay in touch with some of the most important people in my life. We mostly stay in touch through calls, texting, FaceTime, Skype, and Facebook. Although none of these tools can make up for seeing my friends in real life, they certainly make the separation a little easier.

I take solace in and appreciate the few days we get to spend together when our schedules align. Most recently, one of my friends from home got married only *five* hours away. That sounds far, but it isn't really when nine hours is the average. I was so happy that I was able to make it and share in that moment with her and my other friends.

[D]espite all of the obstacles, I have managed to stay in touch with some of the most important people in my life. We mostly stay in touch through calls, texting, FaceTime, Skype, and Facebook. Although none of these tools can make up for seeing my friends in real life, they certainly make the separation a little easier.

Would the world have stopped turning if I hadn't made it? No. But I would have been devastated. So even though it wasn't fun driving alone both ways on country back roads and spending the hefty price for a hotel room, the smile on her face was worth every mile I drove and every penny it took to be there.

In coping with the distance, I've also found it's a lot about compromise. While sometimes I get really homesick and just wish friends would be able to come down from Ohio to Georgia to visit, I realize that it isn't practical, especially given the fact I live in the middle of nowhere. Visiting with them when I go back home makes more sense, especially since I can stay with my parents.

When my friends don't answer their phones right away or reply to my text messages in a timely fashion, I have trouble not taking it personally since I don't get to talk to them all the time. I have to remember that even though I might want to gush about the newest crush I have, maybe they are at work or at the gym, and I'll just have to try them later.

Since I don't work a typical nine-to-five schedule, sometimes they call me when I'm still at work. And while I don't want to take a break at that moment, or even if things are really stressful and I'm in a bad mood, I still make a point of answering. I know I will feel better having talked with them, even though the timing might not be ideal.

While I would like to tell you the homesickness gets easier to deal with or hurts less the longer I'm away from home, the truth is that I've found it actually gets harder.

I know that the longer I live away from home, the more distance I'm putting into my friendships. While we try our best to stay in touch, I know that we are slowly drifting apart. While I know that's not intentional, it is hard to stay close with someone you only see twice or three times a year. It's inevitable.

For now, I can only take it step by step and hope that someday I'll be able to be back in their lives again on a daily basis. Until then, thank god for technology!

U Chic's Real-World Essentials—The Social Scene

- **Tempted to hit the couch when you walk in the front door after work?** Stay active by bringing gym clothes with you to work and heading straight to your workout afterward. Don't even tempt yourself by stopping at home first!

- **Don't be afraid to expand your friendships and relationships outside the ones you currently have.** Try reaching out to people who share similar interests and passions via social media or clubs you are involved in, as opposed to people you are forced to interact with because their cubicles are next to yours at work. Nothing against your work pals, but you are likely to have more fulfilling relationships with people who share similar interests with you outside of work.

- **Dealing with the homesick blues in your new hometown?** Try to adapt to your new city and make new friends. While they won't replace your friends from home, they'll certainly help you get over being homesick (and help you have a lot more fun!).

- **Are you typically shy in social situations?** Remind yourself the situation is only temporary. You aren't going to get stuck in a moment forever; it's only for specific duration of time. The bottom line: It will be over soon; you just have to pull through it.

- **In stressful social situations, keep in mind that people don't analyze you as much as you think they do.** We all make mistakes, even the best speakers among us. If you fumble during a speech or a personal interaction gets awkward, it only lasts for that moment. Fifteen minutes after it's over, everyone has forgotten it, so you should, too!

Looking for more great advice? Head to www.UChic.com/Diploma-Diaries, where you will find our favorite resources and websites—they come highly recommended by our guide's contributors and editors. Be sure to leave your suggestions as well!

CHAPTER 5

Dating Essentials

Is the guy I'm dating the one?

Maybe it's time to give online dating a real shot after so many bad set-ups.

Can you really find a good guy at a bar?

Why should we get married? We have a great relationship as it is.

Do any of these questions or statements sound familiar? Even if you haven't uttered any of them, you likely have a close friend or coworker who has.

Dating in your twenties is a complicated subject and one that will probably occupy a lot of your daydreams. After all, spending your free time with someone you enjoy makes life a whole lot more fun, but finding that right person is often not that easy.

So why does finding the right someone have to be so difficult? There are many reasons, but the most obvious is that, during your twenties, you are making leaps and bounds in getting to know yourself better. Who you were in college is not the person you are becoming today, so suddenly you might find yourself questioning whether the perfect guy you found is college is the perfect guy for you today. That's absolutely fine. This is your exploration phase. Your interests and passions are evolving, and with that evolution comes a need to explore your options in finding the perfect partner.

Whether you're in a committed relationship that is headed toward marriage or loving the single life with an occasional hiccup along the way, you may find help in the following essays, which tackle all sides of this important issue.

Learning from My College Dating Mistakes

Rajul Punjabi
Kean University and
Long Island University graduate

My college boyfriend did not just teach me about relationship red flags. He was, in the entirety of his being, a giant, waving red flag.

Andre was everything I ever wanted at age twenty. He was sexy and intellectually stimulating, and the captain of the soccer team. He played a mean game of Scrabble and was a bona fide social moth (who gave me butterflies). He was cultured and bilingual, with a strongly chiseled jaw and a fiery disposition to match.

Of course, he ended up shattering my heart into a thousand pieces.

The mess took years to clean up, and in my late twenties, I'm embarrassed to say that I'm still dealing with some of the emotional shards that the relationship left behind.

However, the heart I glued back together beats like a million drums. It is equally as whimsical, yet sensible and compassionate. It works with my brain, instead of fiercely and constantly battling it. It is expressive, unbridled, and intuitive with keen discernment. So, today I thank Andre for my conscious decision to stand in love instead of falling like a clumsy mess.

We had an introduction-to-art class together sophomore year. Everyone knows that a studio filled with easels, brushes, and the fumes of cheap tempera paint is the perfect environment to woo a potential dorm lover. I watched furtively from the other side of the classroom, wondering what the big deal was about this guy that all the females were swooning over.

"Andre, will you walk me to my dorm after class?" Shannon whispered, Marilyn-like, gathering her bouncy blond tresses over her shoulder. "It's getting dark early now."

Another chimed in, "Dre, I'm coming to your game next week. Don't forget."

I distinctly remember rolling my baby browns. But he seemed unfazed, answering in a noncommittal fashion, more concerned with the awful charcoal sketch of a Brooklyn building he was working on. Three or four weeks into the course, the soccer player somehow ended up sitting right next to me, commenting on my paintings, asking questions, stealing glances. In turn, I stopped rocking sweats to class and opted for my stretchy jeans. I let him walk me back to my dorm, take me out for ice cream, kiss me to the point of light-headed euphoria, and eventually, we made it Facebook official.

> The mess took years to clean up, and in my late twenties, I'm embarrassed to say that I'm still dealing with some of the emotional shards that the relationship left behind.

The honeymoon stage was incredible. We smoked up and talked for hours on end about religion, politics, and our future. We fought and made up ferociously. Even my friends fell for his charm, loving the spirit he brought out in me.

Through it all, though, I never felt completely safe and secure with him—which was exciting at the time. I remember feeling the tightness in my chest that grew as we began to communicate less. There were nights when I couldn't find him, only to wake up to a text message that he had passed out after a night at the bar with the team. I trusted him, but something just didn't feel right. Still, the passion was unparalleled, and when we were together, the entire world melted around us into a groveling puddle at our royal feet.

Andre was a jealous and possessive boyfriend, yet largely inaccessible himself. His temper was a quiet storm, silence his weapon of choice.

Let's not get it twisted: I was not (and still am not) the perfect girlfriend. However, I tried and compromised in an attempt to salvage the connection we first had. As our bond began to wither, and I continued to bend to his demands, I felt the respect we had for each other begin to fade.

And then it all came crashing down.

One night, I got a hysterical phone call from my best friend. She had just discovered her boyfriend—a close friend of mine as well—dead in his apartment from an accidental overdose. While this was the most traumatic and upsetting event I'd ever experienced in my young life, I went into survival mode to keep her going. I did what I had to do to keep her—and myself—afloat.

Unfortunately, Andre never understood what I was going through, even though he was there with me the night it happened. After the first week of mourning, he demanded his girlfriend back in full force and refused to provide any kind of support. One night, as I wept quietly in my room, he told me that I was spreading myself too thin and it was time I "moved on" from all the grieving.

I happily discovered that Andre reflected my experimental stage in college. Our relationship helped me to create a nonnegotiable list of expectations from a partner, as well to decipher what a true deal-breaker is. Andre and I lacked the stable basis of a healthy relationship, which I believe is friendship.

That's when I knew I had to let him go and never look back.

But I have looked back—so many times, in fact, that my future gets jealous. But while all the nostalgia seems detrimental, it actually resurrected my love life.

I happily discovered that Andre reflected my experimental stage in college. Our relationship helped me to create a nonnegotiable list of expectations from a partner, as well to decipher what a true deal-breaker is. Andre and I lacked the stable basis of a healthy relationship, which I believe is friendship.

U Chic's Reality Check

If you don't recognize your own relationship mistakes, you are bound to repeat them. Evolution is the name of the game. Here's how not to make the same mistake twice when it comes to dating:

- **Placing blame on your ex is perfectly fine.** Denying your own faults is not. Assess what went wrong—along with what went right—for both of you, and bring this learning to future relationships.

- **Ditch the idea of having a "type."** One of the most beautiful things about being human is being able to grow, change, and find joy in the new. And that includes new partners.

- **Don't be shy about what you want.** Be honest with yourself and with the world about what you want from a relationship. If you put those thoughts out there with genuine intent, they will more likely become reality.

When I graduated the spring semester after we broke up, I walked away with a degree that proved my tenacity as an intellectual. On the flip side, I boasted a broken relationship under my belt that had taught me just as much, if not more—tuition free. I went into full-fledged player mode after college, enjoying my freedom and refusing to settle, dating five or six guys at a time, eschewing their given names—sometimes out of forgetfulness—and referring to all of them as "baby." Vast and overpopulated Manhattan, after all, is the best place to pull this stunt. I told myself I was doing this partially for feminist purposes, but mostly it stemmed from fear and debilitating trust issues.

Would every guy be another Andre?

Thankfully not, I found. Something amazing eventually happened: I grew, and so did my spirit. I had a support system in my family and friends. Along the way, I even miraculously dated some incredible men who peeled off layers of me to reveal a more open heart. Today, I'm left with what my psychologist friend deems "a healthy level of skepticism."

Last week, over sushi, a sexy saxophonist I've been seeing asked me to be his girlfriend. The college girl in me cringed, flooded by memories of the catastrophic repercussions of the word "girlfriend." Then I stopped and realized that I moved out of the dorms quite a few years ago.

I'm stronger, smarter, and I even have a few gray hairs, which I refuse to dye.

"I'm in," I told him. "Can I have your ginger?"

And that was that.

While Andre is responsible for my slowly convalescing commitment issues, this is my open thank-you letter to him. Thank you for showing me what my boundaries are by crossing them. Thank you for sharing your recipes, your culture, and your body with me. Thank you for your syrupy words and your charm; without them, I might never be able to appreciate honesty and real affection.

Most of all, thank you for helping me see that good-byes are sometimes not only uncontrollable but transformational.

From Long Distance to Living Together

Sara Aisenberg
University of North Texas graduate

During spring break of my freshman year in college, I went home to Dallas. Tom, my boyfriend of about two months, went home to St. Louis. Call it young love, infatuation, the "honeymoon stage" or dramatics, but those ten days seemed to drag on for years.

Tom and I couldn't wait to get back into our routine of spending (almost) every waking moment together. Little did we know that spring break was just our first taste of a long-distance relationship.

When the academic year came to a close in May, I went back to Texas, and Tom stayed in our college town working and taking classes. Spending the summer apart was infinitely harder than either of us had imagined, especially because we were only able to see each other for one weekend during our time apart. Skype, text messages, late-night phone calls, handwritten notes, and care packages were lifesavers that summer, and we ended up being stronger than ever and so excited to return to "our normal" when school started again in August.

> This time apart was hard. So hard. There were lots of tears, lots of loneliness, and lots of dollars spent on weekend visits, but as time went on, it became obvious that we could make it through long distance and remain strong as a couple.

Over the next school year, we continued to fall more in love and realized very quickly that we had something special between us. In May, after about a year and a half of dating and at the end of my sophomore year, I made the difficult decision to transfer schools. It was one of the hardest decisions I've ever made. At the time, breaking up was the furthest thing from my mind, but I told Tom that I understood if he didn't want to do the long-distance thing.

I would have been devastated if he had taken it, but I gave him an easy out. Luckily for me, he told me that breaking up never even crossed his mind. Thus, we embarked on what would be a two-year long-distance relationship.

This time apart was hard. So hard. There were lots of tears, lots of loneliness, and lots of dollars spent on weekend visits, but as time went on, it became obvious that we could make it through long distance and remain strong as a couple.

U Chic's Reality Check

Are you in a long-distance relationship? Every couple is different, but try the following advice to keep the spark alive:

- **Surprise each other from time to time.** Surprises can be anything from showing up on the person's doorstep for a special occasion, ordering the person lunch or dinner and having it delivered, or sending the person a card or care package just because, to anything else you can think of to make your significant other feel special.

- **Remember that the little things do matter.** Even if you and your significant other have a standing bedtime phone date, don't be afraid to text, email, or talk throughout the day. One of the best ways to stay involved in each other's lives is to keep the other person updated about your day—even the smallest details. Did something funny or good happen to you? Share the news! Often, your significant other will be your best friend, so he or she will be the first person you want to share things with. Lucky for us, modern technology makes it easy.

- **Don't sweat the small stuff.** When all you have are text messages, emails, late-night phone calls, and Skype, it's easy to read too much into things. Don't go crazy if a phone call is shorter or less "lovey dovey" than normal. Don't get offended if your significant other doesn't respond to your text right away. Things happen, and people get busy. But if you're concerned, talk to your significant other about it.

To put it simply, our time apart taught us how to effectively communicate, how to be independent individual people, and how to make the most of the little time we did have together. We continued to thrive over those two years, and as graduation approached for both of us, we knew it was time to make some decisions.

When I graduated from college last December, I had a great internship-turned-full-time job at a Dallas-based marketing firm. Although I liked my job, it was time for me to move on and put my degree to work. Tom and I also knew that it was the right time for us to take the next step in our relationship: moving in together. We agreed to look for jobs all over the country, with neither of us limiting ourselves in terms of job position or location. If one of us landed a job, the other would narrow his or her job search to that location in hopes of landing something quickly and moving soon after.

Shortly after graduation, Tom landed a fantastic opportunity that happened to be in Columbia, Missouri, of all places. Staying true to our agreement, I began my search for a job in our former college town.

Then, I broke the news to my parents.

They were happy I was going to be happy—something that had been difficult since I transferred—but they were concerned about me finding a job with an English degree in a small college town.

Undeterred, I kept looking but had little luck. I still hadn't found a job when April rolled around, so Tom and I decided that I'd have better luck finding a job once I moved. We set the moving date for May 5.

Over the next few weeks, we signed a lease, and I gave my notice at work as I started to pack up my stuff and continued to get my family used to the idea. I was surprised that my parents weren't concerned that Tom and I are of different religious backgrounds—he's Christian, and I'm Jewish, that we'd be "living in sin," that we were moving in together after being long distance for so long, or that we were still young (we were both twenty-two at the time). They were most concerned about me finding a job and being able to support myself.

I shared in their worry, but I knew I'd have better luck finding a job once I was living in my target market. So, with Tom's help, I made the move from Dallas to Columbia, from my parents' house to my own apartment, from financially dependent to financially independent, and from a long-distance relationship to cohabitation. A lot to take on in such a short time!

During the weeks leading up to the move, countless people told me that Tom and I would go through an intense adjustment period. I knew this was normal, but we were also confident that we could get through anything. After all, we had survived and thrived during our long-distance days.

Honestly, we weren't very worried about the potential adjustment period and how living together would change our relationship, except for the better. Maybe we were naïve, but we'd known for quite some time that we had a long future ahead of us, and moving in together was just the next step in the process—a step that we were very excited about and ready to take.

I'm happy to report that we went through a very minimal adjustment period. Yes, moving is stressful and often brings out the worst in people, and we had a few battles while we were setting up the apartment, but living together has been so surprisingly *normal.* It's like we've been living together for years rather than 600 miles apart. Sure, he wishes I'd wash out the sink after I do my makeup and put my shoes away when I take them off. And sure, I wish he'd unload the dishwasher a little more often, but things are good. Really good.

U Chic's Reality Check

Moving in together is a big step in any relationship. Whether you're long distance or live just minutes apart, keep the following tips in mind before taking the cohabitation plunge:

- **Be on the same page.** Moving is stressful and can bring out the worst in anyone—even the perfect couple. To make the moving process easier, make sure you're on the same page about how much you want to spend, where you want to live, and what kind of apartment you want *before* you start looking. If you change your mind about something once you start apartment hunting, be upfront with your partner.

- **Talk about the future.** In the beginning of a relationship, sex, marriage, and religion are sometimes considered taboo topics. By the time you decide to move in with your significant other, these topics need to have been discussed and agreed upon. When you move in with someone, you invest in your future with that person, and sharing the same values and ideals puts you on a solid foundation.

- **Do some soul searching before you make the decision to move in with your significant other.** Take time to reflect on whether you'll be happy once you take the plunge. After all, you can only be happy with someone when you're truly happy with yourself.

Tom's my best friend, and living together continues to show me that we're in it for the long haul. One thing that I love about our living situation now is that we make it a point to enjoy our evenings and weekends together. Sometimes work gets in the way (did I mention that I landed a great job just two days after I moved?), but we always try to make the most of our time together—something that I fully attribute to our long-distance days.

One thing that I love about our living situation now is that we make it a point to enjoy our evenings and weekends together. Sometimes work gets in the way (did I mention that I landed a great job just two days after I moved?), but we always try to make the most of our time together—something that I fully attribute to our long-distance days.

And because we're asked on a fairly regular basis by friends and strangers alike, I'll answer the million-dollar question: Yes, it's just a matter of time before we tie the knot. It's something we've talked about in depth, and I'm sure it'll happen in the next year or two.

I'll be the first to say that every day is a learning experience for us. You can't go from living more than 600 miles away from a person to living in a two-bedroom apartment with him without a few hiccups, but the key is to not make yourself crazy anticipating those hiccups and to not blow them out of proportion when they do occur.

Living together is a serious investment in your future as a couple, and it can be truly wonderful when you're in love, you're prepared, and you have a little faith.

Workplace Hookups: Why It Didn't Work Out for Me

Maggie Grainger
San Diego State University graduate

I was so excited when I first moved to San Francisco and landed a job at a hot, up-and-coming daily deals start-up. It was unlike any job I had ever had—everyone worked hard and played hard, a mentality I embraced right away. Working late hours, our motley crew would bond over analytics data and brews at the corner bar. Happy hours were encouraged, and everyone believed in the cause. It was exciting and fun, and everyone quickly became very, very close.

The next morning he wasn't in a hurry to leave. We laughed and watched YouTube clips and exchanged numbers. The second he left, I squealed like a middle-schooler and started dancing around my room. But then reality set in—I had just crossed a major work line.

I had noticed Bryce, a handsome, all-American sales rep, the first week on the job. Little did I know it at the time, but he had his sights set on me as well. Fate would finally bring us together one night at a coworker's '80s party. Bryce was dressed up as Marty McFly, and I wore an embarrassingly oversized sweatshirt that lacked any sort of sex appeal. We started talking, and before you could say "Jameson is never a good idea," we were in a taxi and on our way to my house.

The next morning he wasn't in a hurry to leave. We laughed and watched YouTube clips and exchanged numbers. The second he left, I squealed like a middle-schooler and started dancing around my room. But then reality set in—I had just crossed a major work line. What would happen when we were face to face come Monday? Was this just a one-time thing? Would we just pretend nothing had ever happened? My coworkers at my last job had been twelve girls and a gay guy, so hooking up with a coworker was completely new territory for me. I was nervous, scared, and excited about the Pandora's box I had just opened.

He texted me within hours and I instantly felt more at ease, but that Monday was still awkward. I could barely make eye contact with him or I would blush like a twelve-year-old meeting Justin Bieber. When we crossed paths going to the restrooms, I stammered out some dumb line and ran away. I didn't know what the heck had happened to me.

He called me that night, laughing at my obvious discomfort, and from then on, we were inseparable—in secret. We'd chat online all the time and come up with projects to do together at work, or we'd come up with excuses to work privately in conference rooms together. No one knew that come Friday we would hit the town, exploring Polk Street, North Beach, and the Mission before inevitably ending up at someone's house in our own little world.

Bryce kept telling me that we needed to keep our little affair a secret and I agreed. Start-ups are notoriously gossipy, and word travels fast. I didn't want to taint what we had by having everyone else getting up in our business.

"You're my little secret," he would tell me while closing big national sales deals that I would end up writing about. "I know you wore that dress just for me today. Why are you teasing me when you know I have to work?"

I loved the constant attention, but soon, like anyone who's deep into a crush, I had to tell someone. Jenn was another national sales rep who worked closely with Bryce, and I couldn't wait to spill the beans. I had hoped she might say that he had been talking about me or something girly like that.

Instead, her face dropped.

"You do know he's seeing social-media Monica," she said. "What a prick. I can't believe him. And he's always whining to me about trying to get back with his ex. He's a mess."

My heart stopped. Were we talking about the same person? How could he be dating Monica when we were talking on the phone for hours and hours after work and going out every weekend? It couldn't be true.

Later that night, he called me and came clean. He said they had hooked up once or twice before I started at the company. She was crazy in love with him, but nothing was going on. I took his word for it but kept my distance for a while after that.

A half an hour later, social-media Monica was at my desk, hints of tears in her eyes. "Can we talk?" she whimpered.

We went outside, and she lit up a cigarette and started going on and on about how she and Bryce were in love. Even though they weren't dating per se, she said they had a pact to not hook up with others at work.

I stared at her in disbelief and told her I had no idea what was going on and that she needed to take it up with Bryce.

Later that night, he called me and came clean. He said they had hooked up once or twice before I had started at the company. She was crazy in love with him, but nothing was going on. I took his word for it but kept my distance for a while after that.

U Chic's Reality Check

Tempted to enter into a workplace relationship?

- **Make sure you and your crush have open lines of communication and you both know where you stand in the relationship, both at work and outside of it.**
- **Set clear workplace boundaries.** Avoid overt flirting or physical contact that could be seen as inappropriate or might make your coworkers feel uncomfortable.

- **Tread lightly before taking the work relationship plunge.** Think of your worst breakup ever, and imagine what it would feel like to have to see that person every day in order to get a paycheck. Ask yourself if you're willing to risk it. If you are, good luck and have fun.

Soon our friendship resumed. We didn't hook up as much, but we still found ways to do things together. He was the first person I called when I found out my mom was really sick, and he cried on my shoulder when his grandpa died. Monica was constantly around and he worked with her. The two of them had to work together and I had to deal, but I didn't like the jealous feelings that would start to boil up inside.

Then about three months after Monica confronted me at work, the drunk dials started. She would leave long messages about how she and Bryce were meant to be, pleading to know the details of our hookups and wanting to know how I could be friends with someone like Bryce.

I would ignore the calls or deny everything, but at work I would be met with icy stares one day or fake invites the next to happy hours where Monica would corner me and try to extract information about my relationship with Bryce.

And then Bryce got fired and everything changed.

Or so I thought.

I was a mess at first when he left—he'd kept me sane at the office, but with Monica's constant spying and attention, we'd only been able to be friends. Now, he even invited me to Napa and I met his family. Finally, things were happening.

But to my surprise, he grew distant right after the trip, and of course, I got mad. Why couldn't he see how this was unfair to me and Monica and every other girl he strung along? I pushed Bryce out of my mind. It had to be done.

And that's exactly what I did. While I still missed our workplace friendship and the chats I'd have with him online, I started dating seriously and met a guy one night after my running club. I was in sweats and no makeup, and he started quoting *The Great Gatsby*. Soon we were together every night, but I knew he wasn't the one. He drank all the time, and I had already gone through that with my ex back in Los Angeles, but it was nice to have someone who was into me without the drama.

After about six weeks, the calls started coming. Bryce was moving and offered me his TV. It was the first time I had seen him since Napa, and I made sure to keep the visit to fifteen minutes. He was awkward and I was defiant.

And then he called the next day and said he was in the neighborhood. It turned out that he had met Monica for dinner but I didn't really care.

Just like that, we were at it again. But this time it was different. We were friends and we were inseparable. We would make each other dinner and hang out for days and days in a row talking about everything and nothing. We didn't have sex, but there was a mutual respect and understanding. People constantly thought we were a married couple, and we even planned a trip to San Diego together. I loved every minute of it.

But like with Napa, after San Diego, he completely shut down. The weekly dinners stopped and the excuses started again. He said he had seen that his ex had a new boyfriend on Facebook, and since he is the only person in the history of the world to have his heart broken, he said I should be more understanding of his pain.

I couldn't handle the whining anymore. He got a new job and new friends and started hanging out with them. I went from being his best friend to being just another girl of his, hoping for a little of his attention.

And then I woke up one day and was completely over it.

We met for lunch, but everything was off. He kept talking about clubbin' and how he got a special ride home from some girl at his new gig. I just looked at him in disbelief. I had gotten over that we weren't meant to be romantically, but I had valued our friendship and now he was like a complete stranger to me. I couldn't wait to end our outing and get to the Mission where my real friends were waiting with a beer and a burger. I didn't know where the fun, road-trip buddy had gone, and for the first time in over a year, I didn't care.

As I watched him head toward Caltrain, I didn't even look back. Instead I blocked my chats, deleted his number, silently wished his new coworker crush good luck, and started walking.

On Breaking Up and Moving On

Jeni Hunniecutt
King College and
East Tennessee State University graduate

Every few months, I would question whether I should continue my relationship with the guy I had been dating and living with for two years before I graduated from college. I felt uneasy, and I knew it wasn't time yet for me to settle down and accept the narrative of small-town housewife.

He made me happy most of the time, but I often questioned whether the life we were making together was the life that I really wanted for myself. There were so many things I had not done yet and would never be able to do if I got married so young and started having children soon after. Things like moving to a city for a while, traveling the world, joining the Peace Corps, or writing a book.

I don't mean to say that you can't do those things while married, because if you have a partner who also wants those things, of course you can. However, that wasn't my situation. We were different. He used to tell me, "I will never live in a place where I don't have grass in my front yard! I mean, I want real, green grass. Not a concrete slab with a square of fake grass." He would never want to live in a city.

We were also both in the military, and although that's not how we met, it was a common denominator in both of our lives. The Army, however, was a means to an end for me. But for him, the Army was a way of life, a code to live by. I wanted to get out of the Army and serve in the Peace Corps. He wanted to stay in the Army until retirement and volunteer for deployments to war. It ultimately came down to the fact that we were just too different.

This realization was not sudden, either. It was something that snuck up on me slowly and discreetly. It would sit in the back of my mind and surface during fights or during those times when I would sit by myself on our back porch watching the sunset and wondering what else that big, wide-open world out there held in store for me. I knew that I would never know if I stayed exactly where I was—on that porch, in that town, with that life. So what was I going to do?

Breaking up didn't just mean walking away from my boyfriend. He was also my best friend. It meant walking away from my home, too, from that condo I loved. Even worse, it meant dividing up all of our things we had accumulated. I don't know what a divorce feels like, but I would imagine breaking up when you are a cohabitating couple feels somewhat similar. It's heart-wrenching.

Breaking up didn't just mean walking away from my boyfriend. He was also my best friend. It meant walking away from my home, too, from that condo I loved. Even worse, it meant dividing up all of our things we had accumulated. I don't know what a divorce feels like, but I would imagine breaking up when you are a cohabitating couple feels somewhat similar. It's heart-wrenching.

I would begin thinking, and then I would think too much. Before I knew it, I would be sitting on the bed in the guest room of my parents' house with random bags full of clothes I had pulled from my side of the closet surrounding me, having just left him. The longest I lasted was a day and a half. Then I would go back, I would cry, and I would give him my deepest, most heartfelt apology. He would forgive me, and although it would set us back a little, we would be okay again for another few months. Until I did it again.

U Chic's Reality Check

Dealing with some of the nagging questions about a long-term relationship you are currently in? There couldn't be a better time for a reality check. Here are some things you should think about:

- **Take time to get to know you better.** Figure out what your core values are, so you will know what values to look for in a partner. It's also important to know what goals you want to accomplish as an individual before getting married and, especially, before starting a family. Otherwise, you won't be able to address the next tip.

- **If you're questioning whether to get married or not, you probably shouldn't.** After all, there is absolutely no reason you should feel pressured to rush down the aisle. Take time to explore how you really feel about this person, and whether they fit into your future plans and goals. If they don't, then it may be time to move on.

- **Ask yourself how many of your own desires and dreams you are willing to sacrifice to be with someone you love.** If being with them feels like an incredible sacrifice today, chances are it is going to still feel like a sacrifice tomorrow. You don't want to have any regrets in life. Having ongoing feelings of sacrifice is one sure-fire way to have regrets.

We never yelled at each other or threw things or punched holes in those green walls we spent weeks painting together. But he could usually tell my departure was coming because I would typically spend about two days thinking about leaving, being reclusive and shut off, before I would actually leave. The hardest part was always actually leaving, actually walking out the door of the condo we lived in together. My home.

After I would make the decision to break up and leave, I would stand in our bedroom with my pink Victoria's Secret bag in my hand and just look around for a few minutes. *What should I take with me? When will I be back to get the rest of my stuff?* Usually I would just throw in some overnight clothes, a toothbrush, and my phone charger, with plans to return the next day to pack more. Then I would walk downstairs, bag in hand, and I would sit down on the couch beside him, turn the TV off, and tell him I couldn't do it anymore.

"I need to grow," I would say. "I just have to figure myself out. I can't be married yet. I don't know what I want."

He never argued about it. He always let me go. I think probably because he always knew I would come back.

And he was right—I went back every time.

Why? Simply put, I panicked. I would try to think about the future. Two months ahead, a week ahead, three days ahead, and I couldn't imagine myself out there in the world on my own without him. Where would I live? What would I do? I couldn't envision my life any other way. He had become such a deep, ingrained part of my identity over the two years we were together. I didn't know who I was without him anymore.

When we were together, I would imagine myself somewhere else, being someone else. I would picture myself living in a big city, picking up a Starbucks latte on my way to my big-girl, successful job. I would imagine myself as an independent, empowered woman, doing what I wanted when I wanted and being anything that I wanted to be.

We had talked marriage and we had looked at rings and we even had our first son's name picked out. We were going to name him Hendrex, and he was going to be a football star at one of the local high schools. I have to admit: thinking about those things and imagining myself marrying him made me happy.

But I spent too much time thinking about the other thing, about the city and about the pencil skirts and blazers I would want to wear to my high-powered city-girl job. Deep down, I knew I couldn't marry him when I still wanted and wondered about this other life. I was afraid I'd end up always asking myself, "What if?"

We spent six weeks apart the summer we finally broke up. He was in Georgia for military training for four weeks, and then I left for two weeks of military training a few days before he got home. The distance between us gave me the courage to leave again, this time for good.

I started looking for apartments before I even told him I wanted to break up, so when we had the talk, I was ready for it. Within a week, I had moved an hour away to a new apartment in a new city. It all happened so quickly that when things finally settled down and I had a chance to look back and re-evaluate what had happened, it was a blur and made my head spin. I knew my decision was the right one, though. So I kept moving forward, keeping myself busy to get through the hard times.

Looking back, I've regretted the breakup sometimes, still asking myself, "What if?" But not any more than I asked that question when we were still together. It's been a long and grueling process—trying to not only heal from the pain, but also figure out who I am and what I want without him. As I reflect over the past year, I can see how much I've changed and grown as a person on my own.

I imagine that in my next relationship I won't ask the same questions I used to ask. I imagine I will be more secure in that relationship because I will be more secure with who I am as an individual, thanks to the time I'm taking to learn, grow, and discover more about who I am and what I want. This effort is uncovering the characteristics I need in a lifelong partner. Also, time by myself is time to reflect on the relationship I had with him. Time allows me to look back on our relationship, separate from it, and learn from the mistakes. I deserve this time to figure out who I am on my own and what I want out of life. It's simply part of growing up.

U Chic's Reality Check

Did you just end a relationship? It can be a difficult time, especially as you're likely dealing with some anxiety or sadness over the breakup. Here is our advice to you:

- **When you break up, accept that it will take time (sometimes a lot of time) for you to detangle yourself from your partner and to feel secure on your own again.** It might even be very lonely at first, so look for ways to get in touch with old and new friends. And be sure to call a parent or loved one a time or two!

- **It's completely normal to feel sad once you have distanced yourself from your ex-partner and ex-life.** Keep yourself busy right after a breakup. Try filling your time with things you love to do, like spending time with friends or taking a kickboxing or yoga class. These activities will help you occupy yourself while you are working through these feelings.

- **Try not to jump into another relationship right after a breakup.** Give yourself time and room to grow. Learn from the past, and allow *yourself* time to evolve into the person you are to become.

Today, I'm proud for taking these risks. I've made mistakes; I've failed but I've also done great. I've learned, changed, grown, left my comfort zone, and done things I wouldn't have done two years ago. It's been a year now since the breakup, and I'm still changing and healing, but I feel good. It's important to know yourself before you can fully and completely give that self to someone else forever.

Young Marriage? You Bet

Vanessa Thurman
Ohio State University graduate

I'm stretched across a table in the back of the reception hall. It's the only piece of furniture that can accommodate both my dress and me at the same time. I've been bribed to sit still with stolen candy, which I'm stuffing into my mouth. One of the women in the frenzy surrounding me thrusts my bouquet into my hands. Someone else swats at the giant white flower pinned to my head, adjusting it.

"It's time. Are you ready? It's still not too late, you know…"

I nod.

"Ready," I reassure them. "Let's *do* this."

I look around at my bridesmaids, my best friends. They're wide-eyed, giving me nervous smiles.

I know what they're thinking: *Holy crap. She's really going through with this.*

Truthfully, I can't believe it, either. But I'm not feeling any of the fear they're showing me. In fact, I feel completely calm and prepared. Touched, though, by their readiness to take down the wedding planner and hijack the limo if I decide I want to make a quick getaway. I have amazing friends.

In no time at all, we're marching down the steps to the ceremony. And in what feels like seconds, I'm reciting my vows. Everyone's crying and a hundred cameras are flashing. And then it's over. We're Mr. and Mrs. Jason Thurman.

I was twenty-three years old when I got married. Not incredibly young by any means, but certainly the first in my circle of friends to get married and four years younger than the current average age for a woman, at twenty-seven. And statistically, even though my wedding was one of the happiest, proudest moments of my life, I'm completely doomed.

I was twenty-three years old when I got married. Not incredibly young by any means, but certainly the first in my circle of friends to get married and four years younger than the the current average age for a woman, at twenty-seven. And statistically, even though my wedding was one of the happiest, proudest moments of my life, I'm completely doomed.

According to the statistics, I'm still figuring out who I am. I'm happily stumbling home from bars, carrying high heels in my hands, and learning important lessons from crummy boyfriends that will serve me well in the future. I need at least two more years of this "valuable life experience," give or take, before I'll be ready to marry. Yes, according to statistics, twenty-five is the golden age when a marriage starts having at least a fifty-fifty shot at lasting.

Honestly, it sounds reasonable. And very depressing. Thankfully, statistics only predict outcomes—they don't tell us how to make the right decisions in our own lives.

Here's the thing. When you graduate from college, all of the people who are there to tell you when it is your turn to do something simply disappear. All of the structure you maintained in your life around credit hours, syllabi, and graduation requirements is gone.

You, and only you, have to decide what course your life will take, what *you're* ready for. You don't have to let other people's restrictions stop you from doing astounding, wonderful things a little ahead of schedule, if you're ready. It's also okay if you're not. More than anything, it's important to be honest with yourself about where you are in life and what you want.

The point here is: You don't have to follow any rules except the ones you set for yourself.

Much to my surprise, there wasn't any great secret to discovering "who I was" after graduation. Quite simply, I found happiness by remaining true to the person I had been my whole life. I was fortunate to find a decent job and felt none of the nagging unrest or dissatisfaction that characterizes many postgrads. I lost interest in wild partying and instead stayed up late with the cute boy next door, talking boldly about the future. (Okay, there might have still been a few beers involved.)

> You, and only you, have to decide what course your life will take, what you're ready for. You don't have to let other people's restrictions stop you from doing astounding, wonderful things a little ahead of schedule, if you're ready. It's also okay if you're not. More than anything, it's important to be honest with yourself about where you are in life and what you want.

I found that my now-husband added even more joy and purpose to the life I was building for myself. As a team, we could take on bigger challenges. He has inspired me to be the best at everything I do. We trust, respect, and (duh) love each other immensely. Marriage felt right for us, despite the unfavorable odds.

Before the big day, we discussed all of our options, but agreeing to delay our dreams emphasized a fear of commitment to each other that we just didn't have. We didn't want to wait until we'd been together so long that marriage was almost inevitable or not even needed.

U Chic's Reality Check

Considering marriage? Here are three most important things to talk about before getting hitched:

- **Money.** It's the number-one cause of divorce, so make sure you get absolutely everything out on the table. What are each other's strengths and weaknesses in saving for retirement, staying on a budget, and making smart purchases? Do you know how much debt your partner is carrying from college loans, that backpacking trip across Europe, or their Air Jordan collection?

- **Children.** The most important thing to agree on, of course, is whether you want to have kids. But also how many and when? There's a big difference between wanting one or two kids "someday" and wanting to have four boys and two girls by the time you're thirty!

- **In-Laws.** How involved will you be in each other's families? What about holidays? How will you set boundaries, for example, as parents start to age and require more care, or when a cousin asks for a loan?

We were eager to take on the challenges that we knew our marriage would present. Plus, we did see some positives to starting early. So much of our future was still ahead of us, and we would get to share it. Why not now?

It's been a year since we tied the knot— no time at all, really. So far, I think our friends and family have hardly noticed a change. We still go out to parties and goof off constantly. We don't spend every waking moment together, and we're not discussing kids.

But in just as many ways, we're already different. Our love for one another continues to expand. We've learned so much about one another that we wouldn't have ever understood without exchanging vows. When I imagine giving up this past year and all of these moments and memories so that I could "gain more life experience first," I want to laugh. Just how long should I have waited to be this happy?

I'm obligated to tell you that it hasn't always been easy. We've already faced our share of disagreements. But we're working through them—like when we're yelling about whose toothpaste is smeared all over the bathroom counter. That's the challenge we've signed up for, and there's nothing better than when those toothpaste smears turn into breakthroughs in our relationship.

I'll never be able to say for certain that I made the right decision. There's no way for me to prove that I wouldn't have been better off making a different choice. That's always the case in life, be it a marriage proposal, a job offer or otherwise. There will always be risks.

But every day, Jason reminds me that he's worth it and that we've shown we believe we're capable of much more than anyone expected from us. And that's an outcome I can stand behind forever without any regrets.

Why I Became an Online Dating Convert

Brittany Ungerleider
Binghamton University graduate

My college experience was wonderful and I was proud when I graduated, but it was also a bittersweet time in my life.

The summer after graduation was a little lonely. During college, my closest friends lived near me on campus, but "back home," they became far away. Of course, we have had a few mini-reunions, but it was difficult to transition from seeing them every day to once every two weeks, if even that often.

When I lamented this problem to a friend, she suggested I try online dating.

I literally laughed in her face. I was even a little insulted. I am only twenty-two years old and am not looking to get married any time soon. So why should I be desperate enough to try online dating? She then told me that her other friend met her boyfriend through the Internet and that online dating is not as sketchy as its reputation.

After this conversation, I called one of my former roommates and told her about my friend's suggestion. At some point, she voiced interest in joining with me. I was more inclined to join knowing I would have her for support, even though she lives eight hours away from me. We also convinced our other single former roommate to join with us. I figured, if nothing else, at least joining an online dating site would allow the three of us to keep in touch even more to share our experiences.

Taking a deep breath, I signed on to the free online dating website. I told myself that I would not actually meet anyone from the site in person, but I would have harmless fun by simply messaging the guys I connected with. I made up a vague user name so no one could connect to my personal information by googling me, and I uploaded a picture where I am standing far away and wearing sunglasses.

U Chic's Reality Check

Are you an online dating skeptic but wonder if there might be something to it? Here are some tips on how to get over the hump of skepticism:

- **Ask yourself: Why am I really hesitant?** Determine if your reason is valid (like if you already have a boyfriend) or if your hesitancy is simply fear of the unknown. If it's the latter, do a little more homework before you completely turn your back on the option.

- **Starting to warm to the idea but still not 100 percent sure?** Remind yourself that it is just another way to meet people you would never have encountered otherwise. Try teaming up with a friend to experience it together. There is strength in numbers, as they always say!

- **If you get uncomfortable at any point during the process, remember that most websites offer privacy options, like the ability to block that really sketchy guy.** Plus, you can deactivate your profile at any time.

I was nervous about the actual dating aspect. First of all, I thought online dating was rather sketchy. In my mind, I saw it as a place for mass murderers to find naïve women. Second of all, dating is not my forte. Actually, it is opposite of my forte. I can be extremely shy sometimes, and this makes it difficult for me to flirt or even meet men in real life. Although I have gone on dates with a few guys, I have only had one real boyfriend. That one relationship ended fairly disastrously, and I waited months before dating again because I was afraid of getting hurt.

I learned a lot about myself from each experience. For instance, I learned to accept that I may be attracted to men who are not attracted to me, and vice versa. But the biggest lesson for me was the realization that dating should not be a scary prospect.

By the time I joined the online dating site, I was ready to move on and give dating a real shot again, although I did have those hesitations previously mentioned. My solution? I figured that I would simply talk to men on the site, and if anyone stuck out from the rest, then maybe I would consider meeting him.

As I connected with more men on the site, I started to realize that some of them were genuinely nice people simply down on their luck when it came to dating. Don't get me wrong; some guys on the site are only looking for sex or are total creeps. But, as a dater, I use my better judgment in deciding who I will and will not speak to. And I send profiles of potential prospects to my former roommates before agreeing to meet any of them, just in case someone notices a red flag I missed.

As of now, I have met three men in person. Two of the men I met for first dates only, and one I met for four dates. The first date was with a guy who was very nice and had similar career aspirations to mine. However, when we actually met in person, I did not feel any sparks. When I turned him down for a second date, he was confused. The second guy I met was pretty cute and I was excited at the prospect of a second date. But, in an instance of dating karma, I never heard from him again.

The third guy was very sweet and intelligent. We ended up going on four dates and ultimately we mutually decided that we should just be friends. He and I still speak on an almost daily basis. I am still speaking to a few men on the website, and I am looking forward to discovering what the future holds.

U Chic's Reality Check

Before diving into online dating, be sure to arm yourself with this essential advice that will keep you safe:

- **Don't give out your address until you know the person well.** Similarly, make sure you have your own means of transportation to and from the date location. This way, if you feel uncomfortable during the date, you don't have to rely on your date to take you home.

- **Meet in a public place.** Take it one step further and do first dates during the daytime. Similarly, don't get into a car alone with a guy on the first date. Wait until you know that he is definitely nice and only has good intentions.

- **Always google someone before meeting them for the first time.** Even if you only know their user name and first name, you might be surprised at what you'd find. Similarly, google yourself (user name and first name—whatever information you give out online) and see if anything personal about you comes up. This often happens if you use the same user name for more than one website. At least you'll be prepared for the unexpected comment or reference that might come up, rather than being surprised or spooked. And a related tip: You may also want to use a different user name for each site to have an additional layer of privacy protection.

I learned a lot about myself from each experience. For instance, I learned to accept that I may attracted to men who are not attracted to me, and vice versa. But the biggest lesson for me was the realization that dating should not be a scary prospect. Men are people, just like you and me. Granted, you still need to be very careful when meeting people online. Some precautions I took include meeting in public places, having my own transportation, not asking the guy to pick me up at my house, and speaking to him online for at least a couple of weeks before saying yes to a date.

One of the reasons I am writing this is to hopefully challenge some of the existing perceptions about online dating. When used the right way, it is a wonderful way of meeting new people you never would have met otherwise. Although I am still single, I do not regret any of my online dating experiences and am still actively searching on the site for men I may be compatible with. I am not necessarily expecting to find true love, but I am looking forward to the new experiences that await me.

Breaking Off the Engagement

Deborah Musolff
Pennsylvania State University graduate

"I love you so much, Deborah. I just don't know if you're 'The One.' It kills me to do this, but I have to let you go."

I was sitting on the edge of my fiancé's bed while he watched me, terrified, reading this paper he'd just handed me. My dream engagement ring was sitting across the room in a blue box on his desk. I'd never even seen it. I was clutching this letter, reading the end of my world typed on a piece of plain paper. I've never hated a piece of paper so much in my life. I got up, collected my things, and left my fiancé's house for the last time without saying a word.

Brendan (we'll call him Brendan for purposes of anonymity) was more than my fiancé and lover; he was my best friend. We had what seemed like the perfect relationship. We got along famously, laughed hysterically together, traveled the world, and had 227 mutual friends on Facebook.

We'd met when we were both living in L.A. I was a singer-songwriter, and he was the actor cast to play my boyfriend in my music video. He took the role to heart and played it for the next four years.

One week earlier he had proposed to me, and I'd said yes. Sure, he'd given me a fake ring that was way too big because he got cold feet when he was about to buy the real one, and the proposal was in a hurry with no real planning, but I figured this was normal for guys. After all, the men in my family got freaked out before they tied the knot, and they all ended up happily married.

The Saturday afternoon in January when Brendan ended our engagement, the hardest, most defining, and ultimately, most amazing and awesome stage of my life began.

At first, living without Brendan was like living without my heartbeat. I didn't even realize how much a part of me he had become or how much of myself I had defined through him. "The breakup diet" dissolved 22 pounds off my already slim frame in no time, and I had no clue what to do next. My music career had not gotten to the point I wanted it to, and the man I thought I was going to marry and move to Australia with was gone. My plan had changed, and I didn't know how to function without a plan.

Finally, after weeks of being down, I couldn't take it anymore. I said a dramatic prayer asking for answers, and I fell asleep. The next day, the answers started rolling in.

Everything pointed to me moving to Sydney, Australia, without Brendan. There were so many signs that I couldn't even count them. So six weeks later, I went.

The next year was the most incredible year of my life. I sold everything I owned, and with the help of a bold friend who suddenly decided to come with me, I moved across the world to Australia. When I arrived, I registered at some temp agencies and all offered me a job as a recruiter for their firm. I ended up discovering a dream career as a headhunter at a specialist creative agency.

I met friends. I met the best friends I could possibly have imagined.

I traveled. I went to Bali, the north and south islands of New Zealand, and all through Australia.

I learned to surf. I joined a volleyball league. And I met lots of cute boys and remembered what it was like to feel butterflies and new love again.

Ten months after I got to Australia, Brendan moved here, too, just minutes from me. Lots of people ask me why he came, and he claims that it was because it had been our plan all along. I guess I'll never know for sure. When he arrived, he came to see me, and it was like a switch had been flipped. I didn't feel the same for him at all. It was familiar and strange, but I realized just how much I had changed—or maybe how much I'd come to find who I really was all along.

U Chic's Reality Check

Are you going through relationship woes?

- **It might be time to take a break.** Too scared to do it? "Try on" a decision for a day. Imagine wholeheartedly that you are no longer with your boyfriend or fiancé—and take that day off from contacting him. Then the next day, imagine you've just gotten engaged, and you're about to be with that person forever. How do you feel? Write down your thoughts and feelings as honestly as possible on both days. Don't censor your writing or feel guilty for being honest with yourself. It's much better to figure things out while you're dating than after the wedding day.

- **Imagine a friend of yours being in your exact position**. What would you tell her? Now give yourself the same advice, and follow it. The advantage to doing this yourself, as opposed to just asking for advice from a friend, is that you are the only one who knows every detail of the relationship, and therefore you can make the best decision. Meet new people and try new things.

- **Spending time working on yourself and finding what you love will not only make you more attractive to potential partners, but also make you feel great and open doors to all kinds of new adventures.**

- **Do your best to not worry about what everyone else is doing.** This is *your* journey, and what's meant for you will not pass you by.

I realized in my time apart from him—from being alone, reading my old journals, and from dating new guys—that Brendan wasn't the right man for me at all. He was a great guy, but I was not myself with him. I had tried so hard to make my life fit the pattern I wanted it to that I had almost married someone for whom I had doubted my feelings all along. I could never quite place it, but I realized there always had been a bit of doubt—the same doubt that made him break off the engagement.

I realized in my time apart from him—from being alone, reading my old journals, and from dating new guys—that Brendan wasn't the right man for me at all. He was a great guy, but I was not myself with him. I had tried so hard to make my life fit the pattern I wanted it to that I had almost married someone for whom I had doubted my feelings all along.

I promised myself then and there that I will never settle. Through dating other guys, I am finding out what things are essential to me in a relationship, what are deal breakers, and what are not that big of a deal. But I simply cannot and will not marry someone if I feel any bit of doubt about them. Sometimes, it's hard being thirty-two and not engaged or married with kids, but I realize that I don't want to get married just to get married. I want to be madly in love with my husband and so excited to spend the rest of my life with him. I believe everyone deserves that, and I'll wait for that this time.

In the meanwhile, I'm having the time of my life. I'm going to exotic places and entertaining fabulous people, and most of all, I'm being true to myself and living a life that I love.

U Chic's Real-World Essentials—Dating Essentials

- **If you don't recognize your own relationship mistakes, you are bound to repeat them.** Evolution is the name of the game. Placing blame on your ex is perfectly fine. Denying your own faults is not. Assess what went wrong—along with what went right—for both of you, and bring this learning to future relationships.

- **Tempted to enter into a workplace relationship?** Tread lightly before taking the work relationship plunge. Think of your worst breakup ever, and imagine how it would feel to have to see that person every day in order to get a paycheck. Ask yourself if you're willing to risk it. If you are, good luck and have fun.

- **Wondering whether the long-term relationship you are in is worth staying in?** Take time to get to know *you* better. Figure out what your core values are, so you will know what values to look for in a partner. It's also important to know what goals you want to accomplish as an individual before getting married and, especially, before starting a family.

- **If you're questioning whether or not to get married to someone, you probably shouldn't.** After all, there is absolutely no reason you should feel pressured to rush down the aisle. Take time to explore how you really feel about this person, and whether they fit into your future plans and goals. If they don't, then it may be time to move on.

- **Are you in a long-distance relationship?** Don't sweat the small stuff. When all you have are text messages, emails, late-night phone calls, and Skype, it's easy to read too much into things. Don't go crazy if a phone call is shorter or less "lovey dovey" than normal. Don't get offended if your significant other doesn't respond to your text right away. Things happen, and people get busy. But if you're concerned, talk to your significant other about it.

Looking for more great advice? Head to www.UChic.com/Diploma-Diaries, where you will find our favorite resources and websites—they come highly recommended by our guide's contributors and editors. Be sure to leave your suggestions as well!

CHAPTER 6

Doing Things That Matter

In the postcollege world, you are in charge of your life.

From work time to play time, there is no one that you have to answer to (well, maybe except for your boss). If you have a job, outside of those work hours, your free time is entirely in your control. So it's no surprise that another big challenge you'll face after college is deciding how you are going to spend your free time now that all of those college activities and meetings that filled your weekly schedule are long gone.

Not knowing how you are going to fill that free time can be disconcerting. After all, no matter how involved or important you were in college, in the real world, you're essentially starting over, working to find meaning and relevance for yourself in the postcollege world. No matter how you choose to spend your free time these days, hopefully, you are doing things that matter to you, whether they are helping you grow socially, personally, or professionally.

One of the most fulfilling things I've done since college graduation is to reconnect with those childhood activities that I didn't have time for in college. For instance, I was a big music geek growing up. From piano lessons to weekend choral and orchestra practices to voice recitals during the holidays, I couldn't get enough. It was one of my social outlets. However, since I wasn't going to be the next Itzhak Perlman, I didn't pursue anything musically related in college. I just didn't have time, being so busy instead with various community service initiatives and on-campus leadership roles.

I loved these activities. After college, however, I found myself struggling to find those same leadership opportunities for someone so young and inexperienced. I got involved in a few initiatives in my new hometown of Philly, but it didn't feel the same. Often, I was the youngest member in these organizations, making it initially difficult to connect with the group's other members. Things got better over time, but what really helped smooth the transition was to get back to my musical passions. I picked up the guitar and joined a local choir; it felt so good to be back in the groove!

So how to find *your* groove? Besides rediscovering your passions, reading the following essays should help get your creative juices flowing. And no matter what, make sure your time—work and play—is time well spent and time enjoyed. It would be a waste if it were otherwise. Keep exploring the boundless opportunities that are out there and looking for ways to put your passions to work.

Reconnecting with Those College Passions

Margaret Darling
Luther College graduate

During my first year of college, I was given the empowering opportunity to join a myriad of clubs, all looking for new members, all expecting to have fresh, doe-eyed eighteen- and nineteen-year-olds sign up and begin contributing to their fantastic causes.

For four years, September signaled the transition from the dreary confines of life in my childhood bedroom to the bustling life on campus and once again getting to participate in the causes about which I was most passionate. I was continuously thrilled at the prospects and new contacts that each new year brought me.

Through these opportunities, I grew tremendously. Late-night conversations about politics and moral issues in today's world led to the discovery of a writing opportunity on campus. Students were to write nonfiction pieces that grappled with the complexities of a dilemma that most intrigued them. I signed up, and through it, developed an even stronger passion for writing and the power of a well-crafted argument.

Yet, as I grew in my passions, like writing, I also developed a habit called "list-making." With each new club, activity, or aspiration, I created a list of things to do immediately, things to get done in the next month, things to complete by the end of the semester, and things to achieve by the end of my time in college. Each new opportunity was broken down into manageable steps, helping me glide effortlessly into the next step of accomplishment.

Over time, this grew to be a supremely effective system for me. As I checked off each task, I could tangibly feel the leaps and bounds with which I was moving forward. I came to write better, read more literary articles, stay on top of the news, and participate in more extracurricular activities. All I had to do was create a list and check off the boxes as I went.

"Would life after college operate so perfectly in the same way?" I wondered at the time. Little did I know I was bound for disaster.

As I embarked on the new adventure that is "The Real World" (not the MTV version), I brought along these same box-checking practices and memories of their subsequent successes. I bought new notebooks and planners to keep myself on schedule and started creating lists. Lists of jobs for which I intended to apply. Lists of book clubs in the area that I'd like to join. Lists of news sources that I should read each day. Lists of events coming up in my city. Lists of organizations I could work with to keep up on my Spanish. And the lists went on and on.

As I checked off each task, I could tangibly feel the leaps and bounds with which I was moving forward. I came to write better, read more literary articles, stay on top of the news, and participate in more extracurricular activities. All I had to do was create a list and check off the boxes as I went. "Would life after college operate so perfectly in the same way?" I wondered at the time. Little did I know I was bound for disaster.

Somewhere, among all of these activities, I would find others that I can join and engage with them in our common passions, I believed.

Yet what I came to find was that my passions didn't always fit nicely and neatly into those of any formal group as they had in college.

Suddenly, I found myself at an impasse. As I told a close friend while aimlessly sitting on a downtown park bench one day: "I'm lost without clear groups I can join, tasks I can complete, and activities I can participate in. I don't know what to do with myself or where to spend my time. I feel like there's so much I *could* be doing, but with no real direction, I feel like I can't fully do anything!"

U Chic's Reality Check

While it may be tempting to clutter your life with things just to keep busy after college, it will prevent you from figuring out what you *really want to do*. Try instead to:

- **Regularly set aside time to reflect on what you are passionate about and genuinely like doing.**

- **Write down your goals in life and get involved in activities and groups that support those goals.**

- **Recognize and respect your limits.** Although you'd love to pour endless hours into volunteering, extracurricular activities, and time with friends, know when you need to switch gears and when you might need to take some time off.

- **Resist the temptation to join every single club or organization that interests you.** People notice and appreciate the person who regularly attends and is fully engaged in the group, not scrambling to catch up because they have a million other things on their plate.

I quickly realized that finding my path in the real world is very different from in college and much harder than I had ever imagined. It wasn't as simple as making a list and checking off those perfectly planned boxes. In college, I had taken for granted the ease with which I was able to connect with my peers in clubs and causes we were passionate about. However, in flooding myself with new responsibilities for each of the clubs I joined, I denied myself the possibility of creating my own opportunities. In the real world, there are so many ways to spend and fill our time that choosing the right opportunities is more than half the battle.

While I longed to return to my collegiate days when I was able to tap into opportunities and organizations that had been set up and ready for my involvement, I began slowly to see how I might use the lack of a ready structure to my advantage in the real world. Instead of being an impediment, the absence of established groups provided me with the freedom to really focus and hone in on my passions. Through this shift in perspective, I was able to see not just the day-to-day activities, but the big picture and how I really wanted to be spending my time.

So while I continued to make my to-do lists, I shortened them, freeing up more time to think about how I really wanted to become involved in something that would generate that same sense of passion I had in college.

So while I continued to make my to-do lists, I shortened them, freeing up more time to think about how I really wanted to become involved in something that would generate that same sense of passion I had in college.

Having fallen in love with writing in college and now lacking many meaningful outlets that allowed me to do it, I began to formulate a plan to create my own website. I collaborated with several writer friends from college on the endeavor, and we are now in the process of launching our own online platform where we—and other passionate writers—can share our cultural commentary with the world. With each cross-country call, our collective excitement for the website builds—a feeling that my former lonely, box-checking self deeply appreciates.

U Chic's Reality Check

Did you find something you are really excited about doing? Once you're certain, don't be afraid to dive in and throw all your energies into it.

- **Keep an ongoing "investigative journal" of research, thoughts, and real-life experiences related to the topic.** Maintaining constant thought and reflection on your passions has the tremendous power to propel you forward in your knowledge of the issue.

- **Don't be afraid to reach out to peers or even superiors for advice and guidance.**

- **Be open to new ideas and concepts.** If this is truly a passion that is going to last, there will always be benefit in considering the merits of new approaches.

A Trip of a Lifetime

Megan Anhalt
University of Southern California graduate

I was definitely that person who always stuck to the plan.

In high school, I studied hard so I could get into a good college. In college, I jumped from internship to internship until I found one that would become a great job.

> Things don't always go the way you plan. And sometimes you need a little push to step back and discover who you really want to be instead of who you think you should become. For me, this moment came a few years after college. I had all the stuff anyone could hope for: a great job, a great apartment, and awesome friends. But I was stretched beyond my usual limits working at an incredibly stressful spot.

I got that job and, after graduating from college on a Friday, was in the office full time by the following Monday. I wasn't going to leave anything up to chance.

But things don't always go the way you plan. Sometimes you need a little push to step back and discover who you really want to be instead of who you think you should become.

For me, this moment came a few years after college. I had all the stuff anyone could hope for: a great job, a great apartment, and awesome friends. But I was stretched beyond my usual limits working at an incredibly stressful spot.

I was approaching a breaking point when something interesting happened. My roommate, Deb, came home from the holiday break devastated by a broken engagement. That's when something clicked.

I wanted to do something drastic to change our lives for the better, and a few weeks later, I got my chance. After a chat with my boss, I sent Deb an enthusiastic text: "Great news! I got fired today :)" And I meant it; I was stoked.

I mean, technically, I wasn't really fired. But that didn't matter—I knew it would make her smile. More importantly, it made me smile. I was free to take on new challenges, to step back from the day-to-day slump and do something exciting.

When I got home that night, I was buzzing. Deb and I threw on our bathing suits, grabbed a bottle of champagne, and headed to the spa. We sat amid the bubbles scheming about the amazing places we could go—England, Thailand, Australia.

It didn't matter because that night, we could go anywhere and do anything. We imagined how amazing Australia would be with its tall young men with accents, endless beaches, and cuddly koalas.

With each glass of champagne, our plotting somehow became more and more real.

"Let's go in March," I said.

"But that means we'd have to put in our apartment notice by…tomorrow!" stammered Deb.

We paused and looked at each other.

"Let's do it," I said.

It was like I was possessed by a fun, spontaneous new me. We rushed upstairs to type the letter, and before I knew it, we were crouching down the hallway in our towels to tuck our notice letter under the office door.

I woke up the next morning with a start: What the heck had I done? I gave up this dream apartment I'd lived in for years for what? A pipe dream. Was this really happening?

It was. At that point, I knew nothing substantive about Australia. We learned you need a visa to live and work abroad, so we googled the right website and applied. It was supposed to take a week, but we were approved instantly.

Next we dialed Qantas Airways. My heart raced when the foreign accent picked up the line and walked us through the flight booking. For the first time, I felt sheer panic as I reached for my credit card and charged the $1,300 for the ticket. This was real.

The next month flew by. There was so much to be done. We packed up and sold all of our belongings in a yard sale to scrimp together the $5,000 we each needed to get through our first few months "Down Under."

Then there were bank accounts to freeze, phones to cancel, and converters to buy. It felt like no time at all before my dad was gathering us together in the living room for the airport. He took one look at us and quipped, "You've got too much stuff." And with that, we were off.

Fourteen hours and a bag of Gummi Bears later, I set my foot down in Sydney, Australia, a world and 7,500 miles away.

U Chic's Reality Check

If you've been toying with the idea of living abroad after college, go for it! It is one of the most thrilling and life-changing experiences you can ever have, leaving you with memories that will truly last a lifetime. Here are a few important considerations for you before moving abroad:

- **Most countries require an entry visa, so research the best one for you.** If you're under thirty, many countries offer an easier-to-get working holiday visa, or something similar, that allows you to live and work in the country for up to one year.

- **Be sure to save some money now in order to have enough money for your first few months, at the very least.** As costs are variable, be sure to know the current dollar exchange rates and consider differences in day-to-day costs like the price for a cup of coffee or a Subway sandwich.

- **Your cell-phone plan likely doesn't extend abroad (at least not cheaply).** Determine the best local carrier when you arrive and go with a simple prepay plan.

- **Set up a local bank account right away.** Your banking fees abroad (ATM and point-of-sale) will likely be steep, so talk to your bank ahead of time and transfer your dollars as soon as possible.

It was around 8 a.m. when we shuffled our stuff to the nearest information counter and a nice accented woman politely asked, "Can I help you get sorted?"

At that moment, the real panic set in. We didn't know anyone. We didn't know how much Australian money we would need and where we should go. We had neglected to put together any real plan for our arrival.

I coughed.

"We just moved here," Deb announced.

The woman looked at us with an eyebrow slightly raised and asked a perfectly logical question: "Well, where are you staying?"

Oh, that. We had been going back and forth between two different hostels and settled on neither. Embarrassed, I redirected the question to public transport.

We took a paper map and relied on signs to make our way onto the train. I immediately felt like I was in another world. I couldn't just pull out my smartphone and plug in my location as I would back home.

So we heaved ourselves onto the train and off again in what I now know to be the absolute busiest touristy part of Sydney—the harbor, right by the Opera House. It was a bit like wandering down Hollywood Boulevard during Oscar season, and we were terrified.

We lugged our things up and down the streets on a mission for the tourist center. I was feeling queasy, lost, and homesick. In that hour, I doubted every decision I had made in the last two months. What on earth had I done?

We slumped into a cafe offering free Wi-Fi and ordered two iced coffees. It was at this precise moment that things turned around. You see, an iced coffee in Australia is coffee with a scoop of ice cream. Score! From there, our free Wi-Fi let us email a friend of a friend of a friend who lived in the city. Half an hour and a payphone call later, we were generously rescued and whisked off to the northern beaches of Sydney where we lived happily ever after—for one year, anyway.

In those few months, I learned a very valuable lesson about life: You can't be afraid to live.

U Chic's Reality Check

Going abroad can prove daunting at first. To smooth the transition, here are some things to make it even better than you ever imagined:

- **Take a friend.** Who said you had to do this alone?
- **Never underestimate the kindness of "strangers."** Your best asset is that friend of a friend of a friend who lives in your new city. Take advantage! But be sure to be a gracious guest if you're crashing somewhere.
- **Don't be afraid to step outside your comfort zone.** After all, you're living abroad, which is all about exposing yourself to new (and sometimes uncomfortable) things. What you find there could surprise you.

I had always wanted to move abroad, but so many things had held me back—fears of being lost, alone, confused, uncomfortable. But those very things make an experience great. When you trust that it will all work out, it usually does.

It took me about three weeks to feel comfortable in my new surroundings. During those three weeks, I waffled endlessly about whether or not I had made the right decision in moving there and whether I wanted to stick it out.

But as humans, we adapt. We learn and grow, and eventually we fall in love with our new surroundings. And even if you don't reach that last step, at the very least you leave with new experiences and a kickass story.

When Your Dreams Come True But Aren't What You Expected

Michelle Gaseor
University of Notre Dame graduate

I landed my dream gig straight out of college.

When the future I had been romancing for years suddenly, and rather unceremoniously, landed on my doormat in a plain white envelope, I was stunned. The heavens opened; the angels sang. I felt like Nia Vardalos from *My Big Fat Greek Wedding*. Hours of single-minded studying, intensive essay writing, internships, summer jobs, a solid study-abroad program, and a thesis had finally paid off! I had done everything "right," by the book, and it was finally going to pay off!

How so? I was going to be a graduate student at my top-pick European history program with funding, on my way to becoming a professor. "Happy" didn't even begin to cover how I felt when this all came together.

And then the bubble popped.

It wasn't a quick process. In fact, I arrived at graduate school bursting with optimism, determined to be as happy and successful as I had been as an undergraduate. However, the reality of being a doctoral student didn't quite mesh with the dream. Little by little, during numerous happy hours and coffee outings with fellow grad students, catch-up chats with my parents and undergrad friends, and occasional sleepless nights, it dawned on me that something was missing from my life.

I realized I was in a "Stepford" career. It seemed like it was perfect. After all, I'd done my due diligence in picking it. So it was hard to face that nagging feeling that something wasn't quite right. My family and friends, I think, figured it out first. On occasion, they would casually ask me if I was really happy.

I realized I was in a "Stepford" career. It seemed like it was perfect. After all, I'd done my due diligence in picking it. So it was hard to face that nagging feeling that something wasn't quite right.

My answer was always a resounding, "Of course! Why wouldn't I be? I got what I wanted—I'm working my dream job." Winning a fellowship for my second year only reinforced my optimistic blindness. There were always bumps in any road. No dream opportunity is perfect, right?

U Chic's Reality Check

Not content with where your life is right now? It's time to put your happiness and fulfillment front and center. In fact, it should be the highest priority in your life. After all, you only live once! Here's how to do it:

- **Try taking five minutes once a week to meditate on the direction of your life.** Start a journal, and use it to reflect.
- **Ask yourself: Is there anything I would rather be doing?** Is there another way I would rather be living? If so, what do I have to do to get there?
- **What resources, people, or mentors could you turn for advice and support?** At the end of the day, you are in charge of your journey in life, but tapping into this support can get you a few big steps closer to where you want to be.

For some of my fellow graduate students, the grad school life did have that special zest. Even the long hours, intense papers, precarious funding situation, separation from their loved ones, eight years or more of living at the poverty line, and the poor job outlook didn't get them down. Graduate school was their glass slipper. For me, however, it was one size too small.

When you know you're doing the right thing, somewhere deep in your gut, you find the courage to do things you never thought you could.

After a year of pinching and blisters, the truth finally clicked. It took an impending trip halfway around the world to bring my life into focus. For the summer after my first year, I had won a fellowship to study in Japan. As I packed, the prospect of this adventure left me wondering how my life could be different when I returned. Where I could go? Who I could meet? How I could live? I realized then that my "dream" career was not going to bring me happiness or fulfillment.

As the blinders came off, I knew what I had to do. I had to leave grad school and the life I had always envisioned for myself. By staying in the program, I was only taking away opportunities for others and myself. Leaving gave me a chance at a life that would bring me fulfillment and happiness. And it gave others a shot at pursuing a path to their dream job or the funding to continue their academic careers.

When you know you're doing the right thing, somewhere deep in your gut you find the courage to do things you never thought you could. For me, it gave me the grace to say good-bye to the watertight plan that had guided me throughout my undergraduate years and to embrace unknown possibilities—to take the leap.

I haven't looked back. Some people asked me, especially as I began the job hunt, whether I had "failed" at graduate school. Why would I leave such a cushy situation otherwise? They wondered whether I couldn't hack it or if the stress got to me. I don't think that's the case. If anything, I think I succeeded at the biggest test of all. My year at graduate school gave me better self-awareness and a clearer idea of what I want to do with my life. It took me one step closer to finding a career that will fit me.

U Chic's Reality Check

Be open to the possibility that the future may not go *exactly* how you planned. That's okay. As the saying goes, life is about the journey, not the destination.

The best gift you can give yourself is the willingness to roll with the punches. Trust us, you'll have a lot more fun along the way.

- **Don't be afraid to scrap your life and start from scratch, especially while you're young.**

- **Not all people are lucky enough to find their passion in life the first time around.** Pick up a hobby. Take a jewelry-making class. Sign up to volunteer at your favorite nonprofit. Experiment until you find what truly makes you happy.

- **When faced with setbacks, don't stop.** Try to find a way around life's roadblocks. And no matter what, keep moving forward with the most positive outlook you can muster!

Now, I'm working as an editorial intern at an independent book publisher. I chose book publishing because, in many ways, it's a "sister occupation" to graduate school in history. Not quite the same, but just different enough to make it interesting. Both are for people who love books, reading, writing, and culture. While I'm just starting out in publishing, I'm excited about the possibilities. I hope I've found my fit this time around.

Don't be afraid if your first dream doesn't pan out the way you expected. The great thing about dreams is that you're not limited to one. They're like a good pair of shoes: finding the right style and size doesn't always happen on the first try. And who doesn't love having a few good pairs of shoes?

Why I Chose to Start My Own Business

Allison Ehrenreich
Quinnipiac University graduate

In some respects, landing that first job is the easy part.

I know all the new graduates out there still looking for employment think I am crazy, but look at it this way: once you land that job, you have to commit to it from 8 a.m. to 5 p.m. (or later) Monday through Friday, every week, for the rest of your working life! That comes as an unpleasant shock for many recent graduates who've spent the last four years choosing their own class schedule, partying four nights a week, and doing their homework whenever they chose.

I graduated in May 2011 and started my job in the market research industry on June 1. By mid-June, I was already baffled by the fact that I had spent four years earning my degree and climbing the ranks to be pushed back down to lowest on the totem pole. I mean, I had a college degree from a great school. Why was I being treated like I just stepped out of the third grade?

I started to analyze the situation and came to a few conclusions:

1. In the minds of your fellow coworkers, when you are a recent grad, you still know nothing!
2. You have zero control from the time you step into the office until the time you leave the office.

3. When the boss tells you that you are wrong, you have to swallow your pride and ask, "How can I do better, Mr. Boss Man?"

Now, I don't want to sound condescending. I was extremely grateful to have a job and be making money, but my mind could not grasp all that was happening in my life. In college, I sometimes had daydreams of walking into a beautiful office wearing my newly tailored pants suit, coffee in hand, and greeting my coworkers with a big smile. Then I would have a schedule jam-packed with creative meetings with my coworkers in a big board room where we'd discuss how we could help other companies with their market research needs, saving their marketing efforts one company at a time.

Well, corporate life has not been nearly as cool as I once hoped it would be. In reality, I don't wear a fancy suit to the office and my day is not filled with important meetings, but rather with doing whatever tedious administrative task is asked of me.

So about one year after graduation, I have to admit I was getting very frustrated and plain bored. I decided to tap into a hobby I picked up in college: creative writing. I found a blog that was looking for freelance writers. The blog was local to my city and covered events, restaurant reviews, news, and other topics related to the local community.

I started writing for this blog and had various discussions with the creator on how he could better market the website. After three months of writing for the blog, I realized I was participating in more marketing meetings with my editor than doing actual blog writing. That is when it dawned on me that I was actually talented in creative marketing and planning.

Maybe my dream was coming true!

To put this all in perspective, I was still working at my full-time job, doing tedious work for the higher-ups, but in my spare time, I was enjoying the blog and contributing a lot to the marketing sector

Well, corporate life has not been nearly as cool as I once hoped it would be. In reality, I don't wear a fancy suit to the office and my day is not filled with important meetings, but rather with doing whatever tedious administrative task is asked of me.

of the company. On the other hand, I was only being paid a measly ten dollars for each blog post I made and making no extra cash for helping with the marketing. I was certainly moving in the right direction but not quite there yet.

U Chic's Reality Check

How do you know when the time is right to launch your own business? Good question. Here's how I knew:

- **When you know you are 100 percent passionate about it.** Passion will promote dedication to your new business endeavor.
- **When you are able to dedicate at least part-time hours to the business.** You should be able to dedicate at least twenty hours per week.
- **When you are financially ready.** If you do not have at least one year of salary saved up, then you should make the business only part time and continue to be employed full time until you have enough savings.

I remember the day I made the decision that I believe changed my career path forever. I was sitting at my full-time job, staring at my computer screen, when I decided I did not want to go through the rest of my life as an employee. I knew I was more talented than that and deserved to be more than an employee. I was going to be a business owner.

Now, deciding what business I wanted to own was a different matter. What do I like to do? Well, I really enjoy writing, and I have done a lot of research on marketing strategies, so why not combine the two? I decided that my passion is to help companies expand and grow their businesses through successful marketing, as I did with the blog. I knew it would only take one client to get the idea going, so I jumped on the Web, and every day I made post after post after post offering my marketing plan services for an extremely reasonable—dare I say, dirt cheap—price.

Put yourself out there and see if anyone is willing to give you a chance. As a recent graduate, you have little to lose!

Fast forward a few months and here I am today. I nailed my first client pitch and put all my spare time into creating a business plan for his company. He gave me high marks, and with that, he passed along my name to a friend who gave my name to another friend, and so on. To date, I have written more than ten business plans and have brought in extra income for myself. With the help of an accountant, I was able to make my business legal and create a limited liability company (LLC) with the state of New Jersey.

U Chic's Reality Check

What are the key steps to launching a business (even if part time at first)?

- **Create a business plan: map out your ideas, goals, and plan for how you will make an income.**
- **Make it legal.** Speak to an accountant about registering your business with the state.
- **Network, network, and then network some more.** Join a local chapter of an association in your industry. Volunteer with your local chamber of commerce. Make connections in your industry and other industries, and with strangers. The more people you know, the more referrals you will obtain. Word of mouth is powerful!

The fact is, I will not be quitting my full-time job to run my business full time—at least, not yet. But I knew from week two in my career that I did not want to be an employee forever, so I am starting young and paving myself a career path.

If you are anything like me and do not want to be bossed around for the rest of your working life, change it. Start with what you love to do, think of ways to make money doing what you love, and take a few risks.

Put yourself out there and see if anyone is willing to give you a chance. As a recent graduate, you have little to lose!

I Chose Graduate School, But on My Terms

Marissa Kameno
Quinnipiac University graduate

When it comes to life-changing decisions, a thank-you is always necessary, and my recent move to pursue my master of business administration degree is no exception to the rule.

A huge thank-you goes out to everyone who told me *not* to go to grad school as a fallback for unemployment. Thank you, thank you, thank you.

I listened to these people who steered me far away from the path of the journalism undergrad who goes directly to grad school for communications and ends up a year out of college without any real-world experience. Instead, I toughed it out and turned my senior-year internship into a full-time marketing position supplemented now by business school.

Let's start from the beginning.

Six months from graduation, I was growing depressed each day by news of high unemployment rates, newly hired accountants, and the realization that I might be heading home to bunk with Mom and Dad in a few short months. I was comforted only by the fact that my misery was shared across the entire School of Communications as we glared across the quad at the hordes of already employed business majors. Why couldn't I have liked math? The creative route was getting me nowhere.

As a last-chance haul for experience, I took a copywriting and marketing internship at a digital marketing agency to hone my writing skills and learn more about the basics that would launch me into the world of Web publication: social media, SEO, maybe even a little more HTML. I will not deny for a second that it was a bitch working every Friday morning while my roommates snoozed away the previous night's debauchery and caught up on homework. Or missing that week's TV shows. But in the end, the effort and headache were 100 percent worth it. Besides, coffee and Tylenol work wonders.

At the end of my internship, I was hired. And despite my couple months of interning, I dove seemingly headfirst into the marketing business. Through a serious amount of professional development reading and the never-ending support of my coworkers, I had gained enough of a foundation to feel comfortable, but in the back of my mind, I knew I still had so much left to learn.

This is where the wise words about not pursuing a master's in communication came in handy. If I have gained anything from the experiences of current and previous grad students, it's that you'd better be damn sure where your career is going before investing in that master's degree. While undergraduate programs are designed with the realization that students may not necessarily pursue their major, graduate programs are intensive, in-depth commitments to one finite area. There are no gen-ed classes. And a master's in communications would be borderline useless in my current position.

So I waited. And I made the conscious decision to go forth in the marketing sector. I thrive on the constant day-to-day movement, the deep research and strategy sessions associated with any campaign ideas, and the challenge of accommodating clients while obtaining business goals. I love it. *And* I still get to write (double win).

So with a little encouragement from friends and family, I jumped headfirst into the task of rallying letters of recommendation, vetting programs, and eventually completing my application to my alma mater, Quinnipiac University. (Spoiler alert: I was accepted!)

U Chic's Reality Check

Feeling pressure to get a graduate degree from colleagues or maybe for lack of a job postcollege? Don't take the dive without really being sure it's the right thing for you. Here's a quick and dirty list to consider in deciding whether pursuing a graduate degree is the right thing to do:

- **Make a pros and cons list.** Ask yourself: What is the benefit of a master's degree for a professional in my industry? How does this program contribute to my ideal career path? Do I have the time, energy, and financial means to handle a graduate program right now?

- **Talk to your current employer if you have one.** The higher-ups in your company will need to support your efforts, as pursuing a degree may impact your work time.

- **Assess the amount of free time you have each day and ensure that school won't leave you without a social life (and with a mile-high pile of laundry).** It's important that the timing be right, even from a social perspective.

I'm not going to lie to you; it is definitely not an easy process. I work a full fifty-hour week and attend classes two weeknights after hours. Dealing with time management, not to mention tackling the issue of loans, has been a strain on my energy level. And let me tell you, the first time I heard the word "midterm," after eighteen months of no school, I got goosebumps in terror. It's all the misery of schoolwork (group projects, homework, reading assignments) without the perks of dorm life or a college schedule. (Did we really complain about class at eleven? Oh, the good old days!)

But at the same time, I'm learning a lot, and the nerd in me is satisfied with my decision to go back to school. Obtaining a master's degree has always been a life goal, and having the chance to pursue it now—before I get too far away from my academic self and with the support of my company—has been incredible.

U Chic's Real-World Essentials—Doing Things That Matter

- **While it may be tempting to clutter your life with things just to keep busy after college, doing so will prevent you from figuring out what you really want to do with your life and newfound freedom.** Write down your goals in life, and get involved in activities and groups that support those goals.

- **If you've been toying with the idea of living abroad after college, go for it!** It is one of the most thrilling and life-changing experiences you can ever have, leaving you with memories that will truly last a lifetime. Be sure to save some money now in order to have enough money for your first few months, at the very least. As costs are variable, be sure to know the current dollar exchange rates and consider differences in day-to-day costs like the price for a cup of coffee or a Subway sandwich.

- **Thinking about starting your own business in the near future?** Good for you! But how do you know when to take the dive? When you are financially ready. If you do not have at least one year of salary saved up, then you should only make the business part time and continue to be employed full time until you have enough savings.

- **Feeling pressured to get a graduate degree from colleagues or maybe for lack of a job postcollege?** Make sure it's the right thing for you. Try making a pros and cons list. Ask yourself: What is the benefit of a master's degree for a professional in my industry? How does this program contribute in some way to my ideal career path? Do I have the time, energy, and financial means to handle a graduate program right now?

- **Did you find something you are really excited about doing after college?** Once you're certain, don't be afraid to throw all your energies into it. Keep an ongoing "investigative journal" of research, thoughts, and real-life experiences related to the topic. Maintaining constant thought and reflection on your passions has tremendous power to propel you forward.

Looking for more great advice? Head to www.UChic.com/Diploma-Diaries, where you will find our favorite resources and websites—they come highly recommended by our guide's contributors and editors. Be sure to leave your suggestions as well!

CHAPTER 7

Healthy and Happy

Long gone are the midterms, papers, friendships, boyfriends, all-nighters, and pub crawls (well, maybe not those just yet) that may have taken a toll on your health during college.

Today, you're facing a whole new set of stressors—from job interviews to client presentations to maybe even an occasional blind date. It also probably comes as no surprise that your health and happiness are important components of achieving a fulfilling life after college.

After college, I experienced a period of what you could call the postcollege blues. The network I'd built in school was in shambles, with friends moving to different cities. No longer did I have regular club meetings and activities to go to. After all, I had passed the leadership baton to my successors weeks before graduation.

Suddenly, I felt like a fish out of water in a city that I'd lived in for the best four years of my life. "How could this happen?" I wondered. I'd been able to adeptly handle all of the stresses of college, but suddenly I couldn't handle the real world. I just didn't feel like *me*. I turned to friends and family for support to help lift my spirits during this time. After a good six months of mourning for my college days and a move to a new city, my mood finally got jump-started again.

Having spoken with hundreds of other college graduates about their experience postcollege, I now know that I was not alone in these feelings. No matter what you're experiencing during this postcollege transition, rest assured that if you're feeling a little down about this awkward stage in life, this time will pass. Just be sure to surround yourself with the right resources and support, as I did, to help pull yourself through.

In addition to covering what it means to achieve a personally fulfilling and happy life after college, the essays in this chapter discuss health and safety issues you may face. But the topics are by no means comprehensive. To be up to speed completely, don't forget to schedule regular physicals with a primary-care doctor, for one, and to see the dentist every now and then. As for the rest, we've tackled some of the common issues and concerns here that you may face, giving you a crash course on how to stay healthy and happy in the real world.

On Dealing with the Postgrad Blues

Emily Diekelmann
Indiana University–Purdue University Indianapolis and Georgia State University graduate

Graduation is a beautiful word. Whether you are graduating from kindergarten or college, it is an exciting time. All through my years pursuing degrees in higher ed, I looked forward to life after classes, exams, and all-night cramming. Now, I would give anything to go back to those times when life was much simpler and a lot more predictable.

I can say with certainty that I blossomed during my undergraduate years. But that made graduating more difficult than I had ever expected because I had made so many great friends and experienced so much that I didn't want it to end.

One thing that softened the blow was the thought that I was going straight to grad school and that it would be exactly like undergrad.

I couldn't have been more wrong. I was offered a graduate assistantship, which is essentially a full-time job. The one big difference? It pays for you to get your master's degree. Sounds perfect, right? Not when you are working a job that expects you to put in fifty-plus hours a week while juggling school at the same time.

The hours weren't even the toughest part. I grew up in Indiana and my new job was outside Atlanta. Not only was I leaving my comfort zone, but I had to move hundreds of miles away from the life I'd known for more than four years. I missed my old school, my friends, and my life as an undergraduate student.

So as graduation from the master's program finally approached, I felt like I was truly ready to face the world head-on with all the education and experience that I had achieved over the last six years. With an undergraduate degree in journalism and a master's in sports administration, my goal was to work for a professional sports team in media relations. Getting a master's degree, at least in my mind, should secure me a position in any job that I wanted.

So I began applying for jobs in my field, and rejection after rejection started to pour in. I immediately started thinking about my safe zone—school—and considered going back to school for a third time to get my doctorate. If it meant that I could avoid rejection and the feeling that I was a failure, I was ready to be back in school.

I began applying for jobs in my field, and rejection after rejection started to pour in. I immediately started thinking about my safe zone—school—and considered going back to school for a third time to get my doctorate. If it meant that I could avoid rejection and the feeling that I was a failure, I was ready to be back in school.

It took me four months to find a job after graduation. Now, that might seem like a short time, but with bills rolling in and my credit card close to being maxed out, I was desperate for anything. But that is a whole other story.

With my longing for my college days, it was ironic that I eventually found a job at a nearby college. I thought that being back in that collegiate atmosphere might make me feel like I was more at home. The only thing I felt was jealousy.

These students still had time to make and learn from mistakes, to be young and just enjoy life. Oh, why couldn't that be me again? I realized fully just how much I missed that part of my life. I spent hours on Facebook and Google, searching my past life and the city of Indianapolis, where I was an undergraduate student. Call it a case of the postcollege blues.

U Chic's Reality Check

Feeling a little down now that you've graduated from college? You're not alone. It's completely normal to experience a period of sadness when leaving the college nest. Know that this period will pass, and in the meantime, here are some tips to help get you back on track:

- **Living in a new city?** Join your local alumni group, if one exists. This way, you'll have an instant outlet for meeting fellow graduates and possibly making some new friends.

- **Make an effort to go back and visit your college campus at least once a year to see professors, mentors, and friends who were positive influences in your life.** They'll be eager to catch up and can even provide crucial guidance during this new stage of your life. And most important, they'll remind you why you rock!

- **Join a new club or start up a new hobby.** If you live close to your alma mater, get involved in campus life as a volunteer or booster for the school.

- **If you feel yourself getting really down, consider seeking professional help.** Often, the opportunity to talk through your feelings and issues while learning to put a new, positive spin on the situation can help you on your way toward feeling like yourself again.

I started my new job around the same time that the fall semester kicked off for most schools in Georgia. Having been in school for most of my life, I remember waking up one morning thinking I was late for class. Nope. I was late for work. Three months into the school year, I finally realized that my time as a student was officially over.

It is so easy to want to go back to an easier time in life, and I can honestly say that some of the best times of my life were in college. While I can't go back, I still call or text my friends even though I am hundreds of miles away. Facebook has become my best friend in keeping up with old friends. And the best remedy has been the semi-annual trips I make back to the Midwest, driving up I-65 to downtown Indy. Spending just a few days with friends helps me deal with some of these emotions.

I wish I could sit here and say that my life is perfect postgraduation, but I can't. Sometimes I still sit and look at pictures from college, wishing that I were there again, hanging out with friends. But you can't roll back the clock. What I can say, with all my heart, is that those life lessons you learn in college—not only inside the classroom but outside of it—will stick with you forever, and that is truly a blessing.

I wish I could sit here and say that my life is perfect post-graduation, but I can't. Sometimes I still sit and look at pictures from college, wishing that I were there again, hanging out with friends. But you can't roll back the clock. What I can say, with all my heart, is that those life lessons you learn in college—not only inside the classroom but outside of it—will stick with you forever, and that is truly a blessing. And slowly but surely, life will move on. Before you know it, the postcollege blues will also be a thing of the past, as they now are for me.

A Wake-Up Call on the Importance of Staying Safe

Steph Mignon
Hawaii Pacific University and
University of West Los Angeles School of Law graduate

A big city like Los Angeles is teeming with opportunity. The place is like a sea of dreams, where there's a fish for everyone if you work hard and wait long enough. Whether you're trying to be a star or just live like one, L.A. is a magical place where anything can happen. I mean *anything*.

That spirit, along with an average yearly temperature of 75 degrees, drew me to the country's second largest city after I graduated from college. I planned to turn Los Angeles into my own personal playground, and that I did.

From reality shows to amazing parties at mansions in the Hollywood Hills to dates with wealthy television producers, it's all happened to me here. I've lived lights, camera, action. I've experienced the red carpet. I've jogged down Rodeo Drive and seen Nicole Richie sipping coffee at my favorite breakfast spot.

Living here has been an exciting, enlivening, and inspiring experience. Unfortunately, however, life in the big city hasn't been all celebrity sightings and fancy dinners. There's been danger, too—lots of it. Danger that I probably could've avoided had I paid attention, played the game a little smarter, and always remembered that crime can happen anywhere. Even in Beverly Hills.

I picked my first L.A. neighborhood, Beverlywood, because it was conveniently located in the middle of the best of everything. From there, I could walk to work in Beverly Hills. It was just a quick fifteen-minute stroll to the entertainment law firm where I answered phones and spent most of the afternoon daydreaming.

My new neighborhood also included two grocery stores, several amazing restaurants, and a cheap gym—all of which I could and would walk to as often as possible to avoid having to hunt for parking. To this day, I am convinced that every City of Los Angeles meter maid is out to get me. If I told you how much money I've spent on parking tickets, you'd likely be shocked and appalled. So if I found a safe, legal parking spot close to home, I avoided moving the car at all costs.

I wasn't thinking about any of this, however, the day I walked to the twenty-four-hour gym a few blocks from home. I had the usual with me—a workout towel, a bottle of water, and my wallet—all tucked inside a flimsy zipless backpack (the kind you pull at both ends to tighten). My best friend and roommate at the time, Kristy, would probably meet me for dinner after at the Subway next to the gym (we were on a very tight budget), so I made sure to grab the twenty-dollar bill on my nightstand.

I smiled at the bleached-blond front desk attendant as I flashed my membership card and headed into the locker room. As with most gyms, especially the inexpensive ones, the patron is responsible for bringing a lock and key, but I ignored this. I didn't worry. I'd worked out all through college without ever locking my stuff up. In fact, I'd been coming to this gym for several months without any problems. Like today of all days would be the one day someone would sift through *my* unlocked locker.

"Puh-lease," I told myself as I threw my white corded knapsack into a rusting cubbyhole.

I was in my own personal heaven as I bobbed my head to Britney Spears on the elliptical machine. Lost in my thoughts about the six-inch Veggie Delite I'd have later and the extremely hot guy doing sit-ups in front of me, I barely realized that forty-five minutes had flown by. I was in and out in an hour.

"How was your workout?" Kristy asked, as I doused my hands in sanitizer while we stood in line watching the sandwich artists go to work.

"Great," I answered, fishing around inside my bag for my wallet. I felt a towel, some loose change, and my empty water bottle, but no Coach leather wallet.

"You've got to be kidding me!" I shrieked. Not only were my twenty-dollar bill, driver's license, and credit cards missing, but my beloved Coach wallet was also gone forever. That thing was *really* expensive, considering what I made per hour at my entry-level law-firm job. "My wallet is gone, dude. *Gone.*"

I jumped out of line, forgetting all about the other patrons and my hunger, and poured the contents of my bag all over a sticky Subway table. Pennies and receipts bounced onto the floor, as I began to seethe with anger. At myself.

"Calm down," Kristy said, picking the change and papers off the floor. "It will be okay. I'll buy your dinner, then we'll call to cancel your cards, okay?"

Kristy resisted the urge to say she told me so. She'd been lamenting for weeks that I should buy a lock and insisted that I store my stuff with hers, protected by a pink padlock, whenever she joined me at the gym.

"Like anyone's gonna steal your stuff in Beverly Hills," I remembered mocking her. "I mean no one has, have they?"

"Of course not, but how would I know if they had tried?" she had answered, shrugging off my teasing. "I *always* use one of those. Better safe than sorry, pal."

Two cancelled cards and a picked-apart sandwich later, I wasn't feeling very confident. I vowed never to enter the gym without a lock again. This wasn't the safe hometown of my childhood. This was L.A., home to more than four million people of every shape, size, race, and socioeconomic class. Fear of falling prey to my own stupidity for a second time finally forced me to buy a lock for my valuables, but the naïveté of youth had not yet fallen away. Deep down, I still felt unencumbered and invincible. I still had my head in the clouds. Until the next event that was really a wake-up call to the realities of living in a big city like L.A.

One Friday night, my boyfriend and I had just indulged in a decadent, extra-cheese extravaganza over Scrabble and a rerun of *Die Hard*, along with a $5.99 bottle of Yellow Tail. We were in love and feeling safe in our little world, happy to be shunning the bar scene as we snuggled into bed by 1 a.m.

At two, I woke up mere moments before I heard my roommate's voice, accompanied by a few others, as I peeked at my cell phone charging next to me. I was groggy and still clinging to dreamland as I listened to happy but muffled girl laughter. My dog, Hercules, a dachshund-Chihuahua mix nestled between the boyfriend and me, didn't bother barking at the familiar chatter that stirred us awake.

Two cancelled cards and a picked-apart sandwich later, I wasn't feeling very confident. I vowed never to enter the gym without a lock again. This wasn't the safe hometown of my childhood. Fear of falling prey to my own stupidity for a second time finally forced me to buy a lock for my valuables, but the naïveté of youth had not yet fallen away.

Then suddenly, the unmistakable depth of a man's voice brought screams to my living room.

"Oh my God," my roommate yelped. "He's got a gun." She stood by my closed door as she said this, as if trying to send me a message through the wood that stood between us. She knew we had stayed home, but I prayed the gunman wouldn't catch on.

Instantly, my boyfriend shot out of bed, poised by the closed door like a cobra ready to strike, his hand thrust back and palm splayed out, commanding me to stay still. I didn't leave the safety of my covers, but I did muffle my dog's snout, knowing that the shrieks from the living room were sure to get him barking. With the other hand, I grabbed my phone, which was easily within reach. I slipped under the blankets and called 911.

I don't remember what happened next. I'm truly not sure whether I made contact with the operator or the gunmen fled first. I was consumed by fear and adrenaline and the drive to survive. What I do remember, though, is how truly thankful I was that my cell phone was right next to me, charged and ready to save the day. Even if the gunman had barged in and taken us all hostage, instead of stealing my roommate and her friend's purses and fleeing like he did, I had already called for help at that point. I didn't hesitate.

According to my roommate, she and her girls had parked a block down the street and were too buzzed from drinking and dancing to notice if anyone followed them to our front door that night. As the last one staggered into our apartment, a young man pushed through the door as she tried to close it, brandishing a black handgun and demanding that they hand over their purses. The entire event was over in about a minute, but the impression will last a lifetime. To this day, I try to never let my phone's battery die and always, always, *always* sleep with my cell charging next to my pillow.

U Chic's Reality Check

They say some of the worst accidents happen when you're close to home, and if you think about it, this makes sense. We're most comfortable in our own neighborhoods, living rooms, and vehicles. After all, we spend time in those familiar places almost every day, so it's easy to relax there. Here are a few simple tips that can help you walk with confidence, work out in peace, and sleep soundly at night so that you're prepared for anything.

- **Always lock your car, home, locker, or anything else that stores valuables.** These things come with locks for a reason. Use them! You may hear friends from small towns brag about never having to lock their doors, but don't be jealous. Theft and other crimes occur everywhere, even in small towns. The best way to prevent theft and property crimes is to stop thieves before they start by locking up the things you care about. Criminals are likely to move on to the easier targets, so don't be one they choose by leaving your door, locker, or car wide open!

- **Keep your cell phone charged.** How many times have you crashed at a girlfriend's house after a night of fun only to discover from her couch the next day that your phone is dead? She has an iPhone and you have an Android, so you're basically off the map until you get home, which could be hours after Sunday brunch mimosas. Invest in a mini-charger or long-wear battery so that you always have juice. By keeping your phone up and running, you're that much more prepared to call for help if tragedy strikes.

- **If there is one main thing you should take away from this story, resist the urge to chase your attacker.** The reality is that if they were ballsy enough to assault you, there's no telling what else they might do and with what. Retreat and call the police immediately.

You'd think after having my wallet stolen and my home infiltrated at gunpoint, all in the same part of town, that I'd have gotten a clue. A clue might have included any number of things—self-defense classes, fewer walks to work, a gym membership at a nicer gym, and most obvious of all, relocation. But when you're less than a mile from work in a fairly affordable and spacious apartment with roommates you love in a neighborhood you adore, picking up and moving because of some fluke incident like an armed robbery and some stupidity-induced wallet thievery just doesn't seem logical. These sorts of things could happen anywhere in this big, bad metropolis, I reminded myself. Besides, what kind of idiot doesn't lock her stuff up in an almost public locker room? I took full responsibility for my part in that one and trudged forward with the crazy, whimsical, and emotional roller-coaster ride that was the middle part of my twenties.

Almost one year later, I had pushed that stolen Coach wallet and horrifying Friday night far to the back of my memory's file cabinet. It was a gorgeous Los Angeles morning and I had just enjoyed a yoga class. I was walking home with a blue yoga mat slung over my shoulder, deep in conversation with a friend and coworker who'd called to regale me with tales of her third date from the night before. Needless to say, I wasn't paying attention to the traffic that passed on Pico Boulevard—one of the busier streets in L.A.—or even to the methodical placing of one foot after another as I made my way up the sidewalk.

"He was so cute," she gushed. "He brought me a single daisy."

"Sooo freaking cute," I agreed. Where was my daisy? The boyfriend from a year ago was long gone by then.

Now if I hadn't been engrossed in this conversation, I might have heard the man approach. But instead I felt two hands on both of my butt cheeks before I heard or saw anything. I was so startled by this, so taken aback, that it took a few seconds to register. My buns had been touched by a stranger—and not just touched, pinched. Pinched hard.

You'd think after having my wallet stolen and my home infiltrated at gunpoint, all in the same part of town, that I'd have gotten a clue. A clue might have included any number of things—self-defense classes, fewer walks to work, a gym membership at a nicer gym, and most obvious of all, relocation.

I screamed and tried to turn around at the same time, still grabbing the phone so my coworker could hear everything. As my body twisted to face my assailant, he pushed me! I, the yoga mat, and the phone fell to the ground in a tangle. Though for some reason, I wasn't afraid. This time, I was angry. Very, very, very angry.

Without thinking, I gathered my phone and rolled-up mat and did something extremely stupid. The person who had pushed me was less a man and more a boy, and he was only a few yards away from me at that point. He was also much shorter than my almost five-foot-ten frame. I could take him. I grabbed the yoga mat, brandishing it like a weapon, and charged after this kid who looked to be only seventeen or eighteen.

"Who do you think you are!" I yelled, among a slew of obscenities that I'm sure you can imagine. I have never been more consumed with frustration and anger than I was in those moments. The stolen wallet and robbery may have seemed forgotten, but they had been dislodged from my subconscious like a tsunami from an earthquake.

Propelled by these memories and adrenaline-laced disgust, I chased my perpetrator down the street, shaking my yoga mat like it was a sword while grasping my phone tightly in the other hand, not thinking about what I'd do if I caught up with him. Not thinking at all.

While running, I noticed that a car was trailing me. "I saw everything!" the man inside the black SUV shouted. "I've called 911." *Of course* someone had seen everything. This was a sunny morning on one of the busiest streets in L.A., which made the perpetrator's daring act that much more unsettling.

The good Samaritan's voice broke my concentration and brought me back to planet earth. What the heck was I doing? I had just arrived at an alley, where I had almost caught up with the boy. Was I really about to follow this molester up a dark, enclosed street with only a yoga mat to protect me?

"Hello, hello!" A crackling voice shook my palm as I realized that Andrea, my coworker, had stayed on the line the entire time.

"Hi," I said, gasping for breath into the receiver. "Did you hear all of that?"

She had. And she had immediately called the police. She instructed me to stay where I was and that the police would arrive within minutes. Meanwhile, the man in the black SUV had pulled up next to me.

"Are you okay?" he asked, giving me a look that seemed to also question what the hell I was doing chasing the assailant for five blocks.

"I think so," I huffed. Yoga hadn't prepared me for the 200-yard dash.

"You were right to stop at the alley," he said. "He could've had a knife or a gun."

What he probably meant to say was: "How could you be so stupid?" If he wasn't thinking it, I certainly was. How could I have let my anger get the better of me? How was I so enraged that running after a criminal seemed like a good idea?

Though I shouldn't have been so hard on myself there on the sidewalk, the questions I asked were good ones. I had bottled up my feelings that had resulted from the last two crimes, the wallet theft and the robbery, and this event and my response to it were in some way therapeutic. I felt foolish for chasing after him, but I also felt empowered and strong, as if the mere act of trying to stand up to him gave me some sort of control. I wouldn't go quietly into the dark night. I wouldn't play the victim any longer. I had a voice and a yoga mat, and I was ready to use them.

The young man who accosted me is now in jail. A few weeks later, I spent time with LAPD identifying mug shots and was able to point him out. By then, the emotion had subsided and I was able to see things more clearly. Running after someone who assaults you is never, ever a good idea. You might be upset, you might feel like you want to fight back, but instead you should take the free pass and run in the other direction. Regardless of what has happened in your near or distant past, the heat of the moment is not the right time to resolve your internal struggle. The best revenge is to walk away, alive, with head held high.

What these experiences have taught me is that life is about tradeoffs. While Los Angeles has one of the best climates in the country, along with a thriving culinary scene, a cornucopia of career opportunities, and a magic in the air that you can feel, it's also like any other city. And what's the one thing that all cities have in common? Crime. You put a colorful array of people of all shapes and sizes into one area, and problems result.

What these experiences have taught me is that life is about tradeoffs. While Los Angeles has one of the best climates in the country, along with a thriving culinary scene, a cornucopia of career opportunities, and a magic in the air that you can feel, it's also like any other city. And what's the one thing that all cities have in common? Crime.

I don't know what motivated the gym rat to steal my wallet or the punk to wave a gun around in my apartment or the perp to pinch my buns on a sunny Wednesday morning. I've taken a long, hard look at the poverty in my city and the socioeconomic divide that separates me from them and me from others. That may explain part of it, or it may not.

All I know for sure is I can't continue to be a part of the problem. The world remains my oyster, but the seas of life can be dangerous when you're not paying attention. Lock up your valuables, keep your cell phone handy and charged, and above all, be aware. If you don't want to be a victim, don't act like one.

How I Kicked Postcollege Stress to the Curb

Emily Roseman
American University graduate

Anyone who knows the evil monster *stress* knows exactly what it looks like.

Like something out of a Grimms' fairy-tale book, it can creep out around any corner. It's a dark cloud that envelops anyone who looks it in the eyes. Or sometimes, it looks like a paper, a project, a family member. Or maybe it looks just like you.

Anyone who knows the evil monster stress knows exactly what it looks like. Like something out of a Grimms' fairy-tale book, it can creep out around any corner. It's a dark cloud that envelops anyone who looks it in the eyes. Or sometimes, it looks like a paper, a project, a family member. Or maybe it looks just like you.

Stress, anxiety, worry—those who shrug them off with a nice, long bubble bath know nothing of *true* stress. It's the feeling of constant anxious butterflies, the feeling of uncertainty and questioning and possible dread. The feeling of not knowing what tomorrow brings is the most terrifying feeling ever, and those who suffer from it understand most.

I am twenty-two and have lived with stress or some form of anxiety ever since I can remember. My stress is what we call "manageable" or, at times, "false stress," meaning I tend to take on or create problems that evolve out of a smaller, insignificant issue in my life.

I equate my kind of stress to the idea of how a rumor spreads. You start with a small grain of a story, and by the end of your day at school, the result sounds nothing like the start.

I have dealt with stress using every remedy in the book. From middle and high school, I have used food, exercising, changing friends, changing habits, starting medication, stopping medication, seeing one doctor to the next, and oh yes, taking long bubble baths.

I would love to say that dealing with stress gets better, but for someone like me, who would take on an internship and five credits, while trying to manage some shred of a social life, I can't say it necessarily does.

But stress, like many bumps in the road, can start to disappear as soon as you realize what you're dealing with. That dark, mean cloud I mentioned earlier is the kind of visualization that has saved me from buying one too many paper bags to breathe into. A persistent doctor of mine once said, "Worrying and not putting a face to that worry would make you go nuts!" By visualizing what the problem once was, you have already made the stress move away an inch.

> I would love to say that it gets better, but for someone like me, who would take on an internship and five credits, while trying to manage some shred of a social life, I can't say it necessarily does. But stress, like many bumps in the road, can start to disappear as soon as you realize what you're dealing with.

"Compartmentalizing" is another buzzword in the dictionary that we anxious ones like to use. Breaking down your problems—both big and small—will help you realize what is physically attainable to tackle and what is so out of your control that trying to tackle it isn't worth the stress.

By realizing your strength but also your limitations, you are able to say out loud, "I need help and can't do this alone," or, "Today I am going to solve this problem." For a lot of people, list-making can help put these realizations into physical words. Having your issue laid out in front of you is a great way to rank or order your stress, seeing what is an easy task versus what feels too overwhelming.

After graduation, I felt a brand-new stress that I had never encountered: the stress of the unknown. I was moving back home with no job prospects and no idea what the next week would hold. My boyfriend of four years was going off to grad school, and I felt like I was wasting time every day.

Every day, I would spend hours of my hard-earned summer in my room applying to jobs. From sunup to sundown, day after day, I would feel worse about my future and start feeling anxiety creep in.

The persistent questions would make the stress bubble over, rising from my gut to my throat. Questions about graduation, about my future, my career…if I heard this person got a job and how successful another person was, I would begin to apply to jobs I didn't even want, just to feel like I'd tackled another problem in my life. I was slowly but surely eating away at my sense of confidence.

Until you verbalize and have a frank conversation with yourself or the ones that love you most, you will be just like me at my worst: feeling sorry for yourself, driving yourself to tears, or worse, feeling a huge wave of regret for the past four years.

Talking to my parents, my friends, my boyfriend, or anyone with ears and time on their hands has honestly been the reason I am still here today. Support from anyone with whom you find solace has proven to be the best stress reliever out there, better than any anti-anxiety medication! Parents will give you the God's honest truth; friends will be the shoulder to cry on; and partners will think the sun always shines when you wake up!

> Support from anyone with whom you find solace has proven to be the best stress reliever out there, better than any anti-anxiety medication!

Having lived with both minimal stress and debilitating stress and anxiety, I have taken enough baths to prune my fingers possibly permanently, downloaded at least twenty meditation podcasts, seen as many doctors as Joan Rivers has, and breathed into my fair share of paper bags. But talking, verbalizing, and confronting my stress head on instead of keeping it down in my gut has become my new way of life and breathed new life into me.

U Chic's Reality Check

For a lot of people out in the postgrad world, *saying* you're stressed is a lot different from being someone who *suffers* from stress. Here are some telltale signs of the type of debilitating stress that you should be aware of, for your safety and relief:

- **Stress can sometimes feel like a stomachache or heartburn for those who have it constantly.** It's a more physical reaction and can be related to how your body handles your stress. This kind of stress can be directly related to irritable bowel syndrome, intestinal problems, or esophageal problems (like when your throat feels like it's bubbling over). See a physician to discuss these issues, and describe just how it feels when you are stressed.

- **Know your family history with stress, migraines, anxiety disorders, or heart disease.** It can help you better adjust to your own stress. Be mindful not to put all blame or focus on that family member who was a basket case around the holidays. Instead, learn from loved ones by talking with them about how they deal with stress or what kind of stressors they find debilitating.

- **There's a huge difference between feeling a little out of control and needing a straightjacket**. Know that while stress can feel like the end of the world, it doesn't define you or label you as a loon or a mental patient. Talk to a physician, your family, or anyone you confide in to help you feel more at peace with just what type of stress you are dealing with.

Perhaps it comes with the postgrad territory, but at this phase in life, even with a whole new bag of problems to face, I now feel more confident, more comfortable, and more at peace with my stress.

U Chic's Reality Check

Here's how to work through your stress safely:

- **For those who have severe or chronic stress rather than the occasional broken nail, knowing your triggers can save you time and even your life.** If certain noises, people, environments, and memories can jump-start your stress spiral, try to remove or distance yourself.

- **If you are someone who needs medication to subside or alleviate your stress and anxiety, make sure you let roommates, loved ones, and whoever shares space with you on a regular basis know that you take medication.** Have the "med chat" about what your medication does, when you may need it, and when you should take it. This can be a life-saving tip if for some reason your medication is misplaced, or you have taken too much or too little and need those around you to speak up or help you.

- **It is important to understand the difference between how you physically feel when your body goes into "stress mode" and when you are the verge of a full-blown panic attack.** A lot of stress survivors out there will never have to know what a panic attack is, but for some of you it is a constant threat. For panic attack regulars, have easy access to water, fresh air, your medication (if needed), and a buddy who understands your condition.

- **Try and keep some of these items in a purse or backpack.** Bring easy-to-chew food along with your "panic kit." Always let coworkers know if any triggers in the workplace could induce a panic attack. Finally, have your emergency card handy, as well as a list with your medications (if you take them), contact info on those close to you, and doctors you visit.

I have a favorite TV commercial for a prescription drug that features a sad-looking woman who spends her day wondering why she's so unhappy and why the world is always out to get her. Out the window, she even has her own mean-looking cloud. Wherever she goes—on errands, to the movies, and of course, to her bathtub—there the cloud is. One day she wakes up and the cloud is nowhere to be found, instead replaced by a sun!

To a lot of people, this is just a dumb commercial, and they forget what the drug company is even selling. To me, it's like watching a reality show. My cloud may still follow me every now and then, but finally letting go, talking, and realizing a cloud is occasionally part of life, *anyone's* life, makes any problem seem controllable and definitely not life threatening.

But let's be honest. I can't say no to a good bubble bath every now and then, too!

How Not to Burn Out in Your Twenties

Maggie Grainger
San Diego State University graduate

When you hear the words "life" and "crisis," images of overweight, middle-aged men in yellow convertibles or *Real Housewives*–type women with faces full of Botox are usually some of the first images that come to mind.

You don't usually think of a seemingly strong, independent twenty-five-year-old woman with a full-time job, live-in boyfriend, and active social life dealing with her own unique types of crisis. But there I was, entering my mid-twenties in full-on freak-out mode.

I'm not going to lie—being a twenty-something can get extremely overwhelming at times. When you really think about it, the twenties are probably the strangest decade you'll experience in your life. You'll go from being a clueless college student, still figuring out what you want for your future, to the woman you hope to be. Along the way, you'll have significant relationships (and likely some significant breakups), make lifelong friends, experience challenges in your professional life, and somehow come to terms with being a real adult. It's a wild ride that can be both exhilarating and stressful. If your seat belt isn't securely fastened at the start, you might just fly off the rails.

Quarter-life crises can hit at different times. My younger sister had a complete freak-out at twenty-two that eventually helped her become the fiercely independent woman that she is today. People often ask her how she got to be so outgoing—nothing fazes her and she is down for everything. She's the first to admit that it didn't happen overnight.

Fresh out of college, she took a job as a wine sales rep in Huntington Beach, California. Alone in a new city with no friends and a 4 a.m. work wake-up call, she quickly found herself losing interest in things she used to be passionate about. She stopped eating and spent weekends alone in her apartment, curled up in her bed and unable to move. Scared that people would call her a quitter if she gave up too soon, she continued working for one long torturous year before she finally gave her notice and moved back home to Monterey County to regroup and figure out her next step.

I'm not going to lie—being a twenty-something can get extremely overwhelming at times. When you really think about it, the twenties are probably the strangest decade you'll experience in your life. You'll go from being a clueless college student, still figuring out what you want for your future, to the woman you hope to be.

After a year of soul-searching (and free home-cooked meals), she decided life was too short to do things because people thought you should, and she moved to San Francisco where she got a lower-key job and is a thousand times happier.

My moment of truth came at twenty-five while I was living in Los Angeles. Trying to balance a thriving career at a magazine with the fast, unpredictable world of Hollywood and a fast, potentially dangerous relationship with a bad boy with a drinking problem quickly led to my life to start spiraling out of control. Although I didn't notice it at first. While trying to stretch myself in a hundred different directions, I started to break down, and when that bad boy left for good and got engaged to another girl less than three months later (yep, I couldn't make this up), my world started spinning.

When Tristan left, I was a wreck. We had lived together a year, and I'd thought he was the one—despite some very obvious issues. I was always considered the life of the party (which has good and bad connotations), but after he dropped that "I don't love you anymore and I'm engaged to this new chick" bomb, I lost myself. I could feel my personality changing. Getting into work with a fake smile on my face was tough enough, let alone meeting up with friends for a night out. Couples made me tear up on sight, and I would polish off a bottle of wine a night just to get to sleep.

I was a mess, to say the very least, and heading down a path of destruction. The rest of the year was a blur as I tried to pick up the pieces of the life I had worked so hard to build. The love and support of my close friends and family (and ironically, an ex-boyfriend) helped me learn how to balance my personal and professional life and be truly happy with me. But it wasn't a smooth road—there were a lot of tears and life lessons along the way.

My friend Reyna ultimately helped save me (although she doesn't really know it). One afternoon she asked if I wanted to join her for a free Bikram yoga class in Santa Monica. I was completely intimidated (I'd only done "normal" yoga once or twice before), but something in me decided to say yes.

I felt so out of place as we walked up the stairs to the studio. Rail-thin Los Angeles goddesses in their Lululemon ensembles jogged past us with their matching mats. I handed the yogi a dollar to rent a mat for the session and hid in the back with Reyna until the class started.

U Chic's Reality Check

When life starts to stress you out, follow these steps to personal bliss:

- **Surround yourself with good friends.** This might seem like a no-brainer, but it's important to surround yourself with supportive friends—definitely not the toxic ones!—who will be there to talk to when times get tough.

- **Don't lose sight of your goals or dreams.** You don't have to have everything figured out in your twenties, but it's important to re-evaluate where you are and what you want.

- **Make "me" time.** There's always so much going on in your professional and social life. It's important to take an hour or two (or more!) each week just for yourself. Turn off your phone, shut down the computer, and do an activity you love, like reading a great book, going to yoga, or writing in your diary.

- **You don't always have to say yes.** Don't let FOMO ("fear of missing out") make you burn out. There is always going to be a new bar to check out, a gallery to hit up, or a mixer to attend. If your body is telling you it's tired, take heed and rest. There will always be another event to check out tomorrow (trust us).

- **Exercise.** Whether it's kickboxing, spinning, or hiking with friends, find a physical activity you love and do it each week. Not only will it help you clear your head after a stressful day, but it's healthy for you, too!

Class started, and before I had time to think, we were instructed to get into the downward-facing dog position. I kept looking at the others to figure out the different positions, and at the end of the session, I realized I hadn't thought about Tristan at all—something that hadn't happened in months. I started going to classes around the city once or twice a week, and in these moments, I started to feel the old me slowly come back to life. I was still going out and partying all the time, but yoga was starting to become a new, healthy way to deal with the pain and get my mind to focus on the things that really matter like my job, friends, and family.

I used to have a syndrome my sister and I called FOMO (fear of missing out), where we would become obsessed with the idea that others might be having a more fabulous time than us if we decided to—gasp—stay in for an evening (which didn't help with the drinking, either). It sounds lame, but it's still something I struggle with. What if my Prince Charming is just waiting for me at that pub trivia night? If I skip the concert in favor of a *Girls* marathon, does that mean I lose my street cred? What if that cool up-and-coming start-up guru shows up at the club and wants to offer me my dream gig?

I used to have a syndrome my sister and I called FOMO (fear of missing out), where we would become obsessed with the idea that others might be having a more fabulous time than us if we decided to—gasp—stay in for an evening (which didn't help with the drinking, either). It sounds lame, but it's still something I struggle with. What if my Prince Charming is just waiting for me at that pub trivia night?

As cheesy as it sounds, my new lease on life made me realize it's okay to skip things—in fact, it's healthy and there's always something bigger and better around the corner. Don't exhaust yourself trying to fit everything in. Listen to your body and follow your instincts, and everything will be just fine.

Part of finding balance during this hectic decade known as your twenties is learning how to deal with things on your own and to be alone. This is a scary concept, but once you've mastered it, you can master almost anything.

Laundry cured me of this. When I had to move to a new apartment after the breakup, I seriously downgraded to a small studio in Los Feliz without any on-site laundry facilities. I would have to make a weekly trek down the street to clean my undies. This never-ending chore would suck up a good chunk of my week night or weekend, but instead of pouting and fuming during the spin cycle, I turned it into my own private therapy session.

I'd turn my phone off, leave my laptop at home, and spend the hour or two focusing on just me—catching up on a book or writing in my diary or talking to other Laundromat patrons. Laundry became my second yoga, with no distractions and no urges to call or text the wrong people who encouraged the wrong kind of temptations. It was just me. I actually started looking forward to these alone dates.

I eventually left Los Angeles and followed my sister to San Francisco. It was the best decision of my life. I have never been happier, and things seem so much clearer now that I've come out on the other side. You will face challenges throughout your twenties, and the heartache or issues you face at twenty-three will be drastically different than when you are twenty-eight. It is up to you to take knowledge from each of these experiences and figure out how you want to lead your life.

Only you can find that balance—that happy place—that will give you peace in all aspects of your life. *Namaste.*

U Chic's Real-World Essentials—Healthy and Happy

- **Feeling a little down now that you've graduated from college?** You're not alone. It's completely normal to experience a period of sadness when leaving the college nest. Know that this period will pass. Living in a new city? Join your local alumni group if one exists. This way, you'll have an instant outlet for meeting fellow graduates and possibly making some new friends.

- **Another way to tackle the postcollege blues—make an effort to go back and visit your college campus at least once a year to see professors, mentors, and friends who were positive influences in your life.** They'll be eager to catch up and can even provide crucial guidance during this new stage of your life. Most important, they'll remind you why you rock!

- **To keep you and your belongings safe, lock your car, home, locker, or anything else that stores valuable at all times.** These things come with locks for a reason. Use them! You may hear friends from small towns brag about never having to lock their doors, but don't be jealous. Theft and other crimes occur everywhere, even in small towns.

- **Always be aware of your surroundings.** Taking a nice walk through the park while chatting with your best bud sounds like a great way to spend an afternoon, but it's also a great way to stand out as a target for muggers and sexual assaulters. You're their ideal victim when you're not paying attention. By all means enjoy yourself, but keep one ear free if you're talking on headphones, always keep your eyes up and looking around, and stand tall and confident.

- **On your quest for personal fulfillment in life, don't be discouraged if your version of happiness is different from someone else's.** Only *you* can define what happiness means to you. Don't be afraid if your dream life is wildly different than anything you've ever seen before. This just means you're forging your own path. Be proud of that and enjoy the ride.

Looking for more great advice? Head to www.UChic.com/Diploma-Diaries, where you will find our favorite resources and websites—they come highly recommended by our guide's contributors and editors. Be sure to leave your suggestions as well!

CHAPTER 8

Money Matters

There is no better indication that you've hit the real world than when you finally take complete control of your finances.

It can be an empowering process, but it can also be overwhelming, with issues and related to-dos like these:

- Do you have student-loan debt? Time to figure out a plan for paying those loans off.
- Did you get a big-city apartment that exceeds your monthly salary? Time to find a roommate who can share the expenses, or maybe a second job to help.
- Do credit cards seem to be the only salvation with multiple bills to pay and little discretionary income to spare these days?

While the solutions to these challenges might not be readily apparent, this is the time to start educating yourself on what it takes to get on solid financial footing, even if you are nowhere close to being able to do so.

Acquiring this knowledge now will pay dividends as you start to make a steady and decent income over the next several years on your way toward becoming a successful, independent woman.

I essentially went straight from college into grad school, thinking I could put off having to worry about my finances. After all, I wasn't making any significant income that could help in any way.

Looking back, I wish I had entertained a different outlook. At the very least, I would have set a tighter budget and spent less on dinners and drinks out with friends my first year in grad school—one very quick way to rack up debt.

Little did I know that a new TV my second year in grad school would force me to confront the issue. Actually, it wasn't all that new. Our first TV set broke, forcing my boyfriend and me to dig his parents' ancient TV set out of storage. It was so old that we had to physically walk over to the set and crack the knob to turn the channel. Worse yet, we were limited to ten channels, one of which happened to be CNBC—the cable financial news channel, for those not aware.

With few options to choose from, I found myself coming back to CNBC. At first, it was like the anchors were speaking a foreign language while covering the financial news of the day. Over time, however, their reports started to make sense. In fact, I became such a fan that, at one point, I could have counseled you on what stocks to buy and what to sell. Forget the fact that I didn't have any of my own money to invest. For whatever reason, I was hooked.

One of my favorite shows on CNBC was financial guru Suze Orman's weekly program. If you aren't familiar with Suze, you could call her the Oprah of the financial world. During the program, Suze takes caller questions, helping them figure out the best way to invest and spend their money. And wow, some of these people need help, calling in with the silliest questions like, "I have $25,000 in credit-card debt and am wondering if I can afford to lease that really cool car." It doesn't take a genius to know what the answer is going to be, but watching Suze's reaction is absolutely hilarious.

Many of the topics she covered while I was tuning in ended up being very relevant to me at the time. From dealing with student-loan debt to increasing my credit score, she gave me a personal-finance crash course. I can honestly say that the advice I received from Suze, along with the extra information I picked up from one of her financial guidebooks, got me up to speed on what it takes to be a financially successful adult. In fact, you can still catch me spouting some of her advice today.

From this experience, I learned that the best thing you can do for yourself now is to get educated on these important money matters, using whatever resources you choose.

Also, never compare yourself to any of your friends who may be having more financial success than you at this point. You don't know what advantages they may have had (such as no student debt, thanks to generous family members, or a career that happens to pay more off the bat). You are in control of your own financial future now, and with the right approach—like setting and sticking to a budget and saving when you can—you'll be well on your way to financial success in no time.

To help get you on the right path, we have a series of essays from women who faced some of the very challenges you're likely going through. Read on to learn how they discovered their inner diva by successfully pursuing a financially independent life.

How I Live on a Budget and Still Live Fabulously

Gracie Bialecki
Pomona College graduate

What's the point of living in one of the world's most stimulating cities if you can't afford to do anything in it? New York City abounds with activity—art, music, theater, fashion, food—and is inordinately expensive, especially when you just graduated from college and you don't have a job. That's me.

But rather than being discouraged by the limited capacity of my budget, I'm constantly finding fascinating alternatives to conventional activities—advice that can serve you well in any city.

In other words, there are more free things to do in most cities than you could possibly imagine. And lately I feel as though my financial limitations have been strangely liberating. Instead of falling into the same routines, I've been exploring the city in ways I otherwise never would have.

[T]here are more free things to do in most cities than you could possibly imagine. And lately I feel as though my financial limitations have been strangely liberating. Instead of falling into the same routines, I've been exploring the city in ways I otherwise never would have.

Though exploration is no fun as a solo activity, navigating social situations with friends in entirely different financial echelons can get a little weird. In college, these disparities were less present, but now, with my friends working in finance or consulting, things get complicated.

Even though they know I'm unemployed,

and ask me if I've found a job every time we see each other, they seem to forget that my situation also means I have very little money. Dinner on the Upper West Side, two-hour brunches with pitchers of strawberry Bellinis in the West Village, even going out to the bars in Midtown, instantly exceeds what I spend on groceries in a week.

U Chic's Reality Check

So your friends can afford the top-shelf drinks at the hottest new bar in town, but you can't. Don't sweat it. Here's how you can socialize with friends and still do it fabulously even while on a budget:

- **If you can't afford a drink, don't buy one.** Bartenders will never refuse to give you a glass of water, and as long as your friends are drinking, no one is going to kick you out of the bar.

- **Invite friends over for dinner.** Cooking alone is a bummer, but bringing friends into the kitchen can be a fun new activity, as well as a big money saver.

- **Don't be afraid to say no.** If you really can't afford that music festival, fancy nightclub, or weekend trip to California, be honest with your friends. It takes a lot more to end a true friendship than missing out on just one fun-filled weekend.

I don't enjoy reminding my friends of my penniless state, and I'd rather see them than lie and say I have plans whenever they invite me on moneyed excursions. So lately, I've been dwelling in the confusing world of blurred truths. Instead of telling my friends I can't make dinner, I'll say I'm going to be late, eat at home, and just order a drink when I meet up with them. Or if we're going to a bar, I'll bring a bottle of wine over so we can drink that before going out, and then I'll be able to coast along on one or two drinks the rest of the night. But things don't always have to be that complicated, and the simplest solution is to go out on your own terms—find enjoyable events that you can afford and invite friends to those.

When leering drunk men offer to buy us drinks at bars, my best friend and I like to remind each other, "There's no such thing as a free drink." We've learned the hard way that accepting one seemingly innocent shot can mean consenting to a night of being shamelessly hit on.

In my search for free activities, I've ended up at poetry readings, the Adidas store's tenth anniversary party, and an overwhelmingly vast art and music installation sponsored by the Creators Project. Free events are liberating because in addition to allowing me to see things I've never seen before, if they're too crowded, boring, or bizarre, I feel no obligation to stay.

When leering drunk men offer to buy us drinks at bars, my best friend and I like to remind each other, "There's no such thing as a free drink." We've learned the hard way that accepting one seemingly innocent shot can mean consenting to a night of being shamelessly hit on. The wine at art openings, however, comes with no such expectations, and Thursdays in New York are a free wino's dream. Even if you're not an avid art enthusiast, the people-watching alone, which invariably leads to outfit envy, is enough to keep someone like me occupied.

Outfit envy often occurs in my city, and though my monthly budget doesn't technically include a shopping allotment, it's so easy to find affordable, beautiful vintage and designer clothing that it's hard to justify *not* buying that fifth pair of cowboy boots. If you're willing to put in the time, you're sure to find the oversized cashmere sweater that's too comfy to take off or the acid-washed jeans of your dreams. And you don't have to worry about expanding your closet beyond its capacity—these types of stores also buy clothes and you can choose to get paid in cash or store credit.

U Chic's Reality Check

Often the hardest part about staying on a budget in the city is knowing where to find free opportunities. Here are some great resources for discovering the best freebies in town:

- **Check online listings from your favorite local news sources.** Periodicals (like *Time Out New York* or the *Village Voice* for you New Yorkers) often have extensive event lists online.

- **Research free days or reduced tickets at various places and events.** Most museums have specific days when they're free to the public, and similarly, performances often have rush seating deals where you can get last-minute tickets at significantly discounted rates.

- **Use your friends.** Ask friends with connections in the music, film, theater, and publishing industries to tell you about free events, or see if you can get comped tickets to go to shows, screenings, or readings with them.

If you're more concerned about what's underneath your clothes and worry about finding the time and money to stay in shape, fear not. Every city has parks! It's much easier for me to fit in a workout if that means just getting out the door—not giving myself a serious pep talk, packing a bag, and venturing to the gym and back. Many yoga studios also offer work-study programs, one of which I'm currently enrolled in. In exchange for three hours of office work a week, I receive unlimited free access to yoga classes and to the studio's sauna, where I plan on defrosting myself, come winter.

If all this seems overwhelming, it's best to focus on the little things, because they do add up. Instead of stopping at a café every morning, I invested in a

French press. Trying out local roasters has been a delicious way to learn more about coffee, and nothing entices my hungover roommate to come to yoga with me like a fresh cup of coffee delivered to her bed. I have a bike, and while the weather is still nice, I try to ride it as much as possible. As long as I look up directions before I leave, I'm able to stay entirely on bike lanes. Transporting myself this way usually takes just as long as the subway would have and is a great way catch some sunshine and burn calories.

Living on a budget doesn't have to mean foregoing friendships or feeling frumpy; it simply involves a little more brainpower and time management, and a sense of adventure.

Living on a budget doesn't have to mean foregoing friendships or feeling frumpy; it simply involves a little more brainpower and time management, and a sense of adventure.

Although my current budget is simple—spend as little money as possible every day—it is a good idea to have some sense of what you spend. Note the differences in your bank statement from month to month, and check the expenditures tab of your online banking page. You'd be surprised at what you end up spending the most on.

But most importantly, remember that you can feel fabulous about the frugal lifestyle you live and the consciousness with which you choose where your money goes.

A Tale of Credit Card Woes

Emily Diekelmann
Indiana University–Purdue University Indianapolis and Georgia State University graduate

I remember getting my first credit card. It came from my bank and seemed promising, with its cash-back rewards and a low interest rate.

That was almost six years ago. Wow, how time flies when you are spending money that you don't really have!

Credit-card debt has always been a part of my life. How can a twenty-five-year-old already have a life filled with debt from those little plastic cards? Good question.

I come from a single-parent household. My dad had a rare neurological disease that hit him when I was six years old, and from that point on, my nuclear family consisted of my mom, my sister, and myself. My mom, who is by far one of the most amazing people I know, was a nurse, and that alone should say a lot about her character. She gives without expecting anything in return, and that is mainly what my childhood consisted of.

She gave to my sister and me without wanting anything but our undying love in return. It wasn't until a few years ago that I realized my mom had racked up a lot of debt from credit cards because she wanted to give my sister and me the life she thought we deserved. As an adult, I feel guilty, but as a kid, I had everything I ever wanted and then some. Playing sports, we had new equipment, clothes, shoes, you name it. My mom never let on that she was collecting such a heavy burden for herself.

Now fast forward to my college years and that first little piece of blue plastic. In college, credit card companies used all types of gimmicks to reel in students. My Achilles' heel was the promise of free food. I imagine that my freshman year I filled out ten or more applications for a card with the promise of free food without knowing the effects my actions would have on my future credit.

Credit card debt has always been a part of my life. How can a twenty-five-year-old already have a life filled with debt from those little plastic cards? Good question.

Then, after racking up debt for a few years, I finally decided to keep just one of the cards while shredding the others. I have had Old Blue ever since.

As many people know, college isn't cheap unless you are extremely smart or athletically inclined enough to garner scholarships. I fit neither category. I was lucky enough to get a grant during my undergrad year, but it didn't cover summer school. Old Blue officially went from being just for emergencies or for building good credit to my one and only salvation. My first major charge was $900 for summer-school classes. I remember looking at the charge on my computer screen and wanting to die because I never thought I could pay it off.

U Chic's Reality Check

When it's time to settle the bill, it's so easy to swipe that card, right? Don't get romanced by the effortlessness of paying for things with a credit card. It's simply too easy for this to get out of control. Here are some credit card tips to help keep you on track and out of major debt postcollege:

- **Try to keep only one credit card around for emergencies and nothing more.** Pay everything else by debit, if you can manage, as it is directly linked to your checking account and limits you to your bank account balance. If you use a credit card for everyday purchases like groceries or monthly utility bills, try to pay off the balance in full each month. And definitely make your payments on time, because paying late will have a negative impact on your credit score.

- **In choosing a card, shop around as you do when on the hunt for a good bargain.** Visit websites like CreditCards.com or Bankrate .com to find cards with the lowest annual percentage rate (APR) and no annual fee. If one also happens to offer cash-back rewards or points, you may have found the perfect one.

- **If you already have a card or two with some debt on them and the APR is higher than the current average you find online, call your credit card company to see about negotiating for a lower rate, especially if you have a good record of paying your statements on time.** If they won't give you a lower rate, consider doing a balance transfer from the higher-rate card(s) to the lower-rate one(s). Most card companies will charge you a fee—typically a percentage of the outstanding balance—to complete the balance transfer, so make sure you know what the total cost will be and whether the transaction makes good financial sense.

Charging to my card didn't seem so bad after the initial shock wore off. I would charge a purchase here, a lunch date there, and next thing I know, my credit card bill had doubled. Quickly realizing what I'd done, I saved money every month to make sure I brought it down. Finally getting close to the zero promised land, I had another set of summer school classes to pay for and I was back to square one.

I will admit that not everything I bought was school-related, and I wasn't the only one on the line for these purchases. My mother could see my bank account, which she put her name on as well, from her computer. However, my credit card is not in her "jurisdiction" (as I like to call it), so she can't check up on me. All of the purchases I didn't want her to know about went on my credit card, with me vowing to pay them back right away. For the most part, this plan worked, but upon college graduation, I had some lingering debt.

One thing I have learned in my very few years in the real world is the difference between want and need. I can walk through a mall and see plenty of things that I'd die to have, but it always comes down to whether I truly need them. About 99 percent of the time, the little voice in my head is screaming "want" instead of "need," so I just keep walking.

I finally graduated from college and decided to pursue my master's. I was a graduate assistant during my grad school years, which essentially meant that I was getting my degree paid for with some extra money each month for living expenses. Unfortunately, no one told me when I moved several states from home that I wouldn't be on the payroll for the first month and a half, even though I was working. Enter Old Blue once again to save the day. It wouldn't be the last time.

One thing I have learned in my very few years in the real world is the difference between want and need. I can walk through a mall and see plenty of things that I'd die to have, but it always comes down to whether I truly need them. About 99 percent of the time, the little voice in my head is screaming "want" instead of "need," so I just keep walking.

All the things I bought with my credit card that were unnecessary still haunt me today because I know they weren't worth it. Having the money in hand or in my bank account to pay for things that I truly need or have saved up for is more rewarding than a swipe of Old Blue any day.

So where do I stand with Old Blue today? I wish I could say that I have the balance all paid off and am living debt free, but I would be lying. After grad school graduation, I was without work, with no income and just my credit card to survive. Things like food, gas, and bills became the only thing in my life, but thankfully, I was only out of work for four months, and I am now proud to say I'm working to bring that number closer to zero again.

Although my credit-card may say "freedom" on the front, I don't feel free from the bondage that credit-card debt has placed on me. If I could change anything in my life, it would be the role that debt has played in my postgraduation life. Don't the experts say student-loan debt is better to have, anyway?

Budgeting for My Dreams (Even on a Freelancer's Salary!)

MaryAnn Barone
University of North Carolina–Chapel Hill graduate

Growing up in a one-stoplight town on a gravel road in North Carolina made me long for the bright lights of big, bustling cities. My city of choice was New York, naturally. I knew I didn't want my dreams to stay intangible, so I realized in college that I would have to work hard to get to where I wanted to go.

At the University of North Carolina at Chapel Hill, I majored in reporting and minored in eighteenth-century British literature. (Seriously, it's much more interesting than you'd think.) I've always known I wanted to be a writer of some sort, so obviously New York was the top destination for an internship in the field.

During the spring semester of my sophomore year, I applied to at least fifty openings. I heard back from a few saying they'd review my application, but I didn't get any of them. A top magazine said I could interview with them if I flew up there, but I couldn't afford to go without knowing I would have the position after spending $300-plus on airline tickets. I never heard back.

I was heartbroken, but I kept pursuing every newspaper, website, and magazine in the city that I could find. I was finally offered an internship with a small newspaper in Greensboro, North Carolina, and I wavered on taking it. Ultimately, I declined the offer, deciding not to play it safe by staying in state. At the time, it seemed like a huge gamble, but I really felt the need to strike out on my own and go for my dreams in a big way.

After months of being on pins and needles, an assistant editor at *Fitness* magazine agreed to interview me over the phone, and with only two weeks before the summer started, I secured myself an internship in the beauty department at the magazine. I was ecstatic, and that internship sparked my interest in all things beauty. It was the best thing that could've happened.

Luckily, my wonderful aunt and her family live in northern New Jersey, only forty minutes from the city. I didn't have much money, so I saved all that I could. I would walk the fifteen blocks to and from work every day, even in the 90-degree-plus weather, so I wouldn't have to ride the subway. I would bring my lunch and plenty of Costco snacks for my desk so I could avoid having to spend eight dollars a day on food.

On paper, I thought I was the ideal candidate. I had experience at two top magazines and a degree from one of the top public universities in the country. But, in the midst of a hiring freeze, I couldn't find a single full-time job postgraduation...so I sought the life of a freelancer to fill the void and gain experience. I've been doing it ever since.

I graduated two years after that internship and another one at my favorite magazine, *Cosmopolitan.* On paper, I thought I was the ideal candidate. I had experience at two top magazines and a degree from one of the top public universities in the country. Thanks to the over-achiever in me, I had also been active in student publications all four years of school.

But, in the midst of a hiring freeze, I couldn't find a single full-time job postgraduation. How was I to find steady work? Well, I didn't, so I sought the life of a freelancer to fill the void and gain experience. I've been doing it ever since.

Now, living on a freelancer's salary is not easy by any means, but it is do-able. As a freelancer, I make money from a variety of different employers. I've been a fact checker for *Good Housekeeping*, a writer for *Family Circle* and *Time Out New York*, a blogger for TheNest.com and TheBlush.com, a social-media manager for several blogs, a freelance health assistant with *SELF,* and an editor on legal documents for a contractor. I like freelancing because I can pick and choose the exact jobs I want, but the bad news is that unlike a full-time nine-to-five job, many jobs have specific start and end dates.

U Chic's Reality Check

The life of a freelancer can feel lonely at times with a lack of support in key moments. Here's how to make freelancing feel like a real job:

- **Read the fine print.** Before you sign any paperwork, read it carefully to make sure you can take on other jobs. Some contracts state that you can't write for similar organizations or those they consider competitors. Also, make sure the terms of your freelance arrangement are in a written contract that includes deadlines—both the date when your work will be finished and the date when you will be paid.

- **Have discipline.** It can be easy to slack off when you work from home and may spend most of your days in pj's. Treat your jobs as you would an office one: wake up early, work during business hours, and stay on top of deadlines.

- **Never get too comfortable.** Freelance jobs often have set-in-stone end dates. Before your current project ends, try to secure your next project so you can maintain a steady income and manageable workload.

When you're a freelancer, it's important to be prepared for the time when you might not have a job. You could have one or three at once, depending on the month. And god forbid I ever find myself with none at all, so I try save as much as I can just in case. I also have a system for managing my income. You have to as a freelancer. The money I make at my latest freelance job goes straight into my checking account, while everything else I do on the side (blogging, social-media managing, and fact checking) goes into my savings account. It's easy for me to see where my money goes with this system.

One splurge I do treat myself to daily is a Starbucks drink. However, instead of one of the fancy multi-hyphenated specialties, I buy a cheaper canned drink, usually a Starbucks Doubleshot Espresso. At most I'll get one seasonal drink (hello, Pumpkin Spice Latte!) a week. I used to feel wasteful about my caffeine habit, but one of my fellow freelancer friends said to think of it as a billable working hour. It makes sense.

When I go to Starbucks, it's not to read or hang out with friends. It's to work. As a freelancer, you can end up spending copious amounts of time in your house working, so going out with your laptop to Starbucks ends up being a social highlight of your day. So yes, it is a business expense.

The money I'm saving is going to fund two of my dreams. First off, I'm still living with my aunt and her family because I don't want to move into New York City proper until I have at least a year's worth of rent saved up. That way, if my freelance jobs were all to end, I'd still be okay. Of course, that apartment would have to include a roommate or two, but I'd rather know I could make rent every month and not have to scramble for money. I also want to travel to London because, as much as I've studied and love that city, I've never been there. I'm confident that one day I'll accomplish both of these goals—one paycheck at a time.

U Chic's Reality Check

Budgeting 101 for freelancers:

- **Set money aside.** Most freelance work is untaxed, meaning you'll always owe money when tax season comes around. I set aside a portion of my earnings for my savings, usually about 25 percent, so my account includes money for the future as well as what I'll eventually end up owing the government.

- **Stay on top of the payments that are owed.** Read your contracts from time to time to make sure you are being paid according to the terms of the agreement. Keep a spreadsheet of all your jobs and the money you're owed. Make notes of when you sent an invoice and when you got paid. It's a quick and easy way to see what you're waiting on and who owes you money. As a freelancer, it's up to you to stay on top of things to ensure you get what you deserve.

- **Know your worth.** Don't feel pressured to take every job that comes to you. Consider the payment and whether it's a reasonable amount for what you'd be doing. Just because a job pays a lot doesn't mean it's worth your time. Some projects may actually have more value in terms of the work you'll be doing, beyond the dollar amount that is offered.

Paying Off Those Dreaded Student Loans

Ashley Cobb
Ball State University graduate

Growing up in an upper-middle-class family, I pretty much assumed that my college tuition would be paid for. I graduated from high school in the top 10 percent with a 4.0 GPA, completed many AP classes, and assumed that attending college would be a similar experience. Little did I know how different college would turn out.

As it does for many, my first year consisted of general classes, such as Sociology 101, Psychology 101, History 101, English 101, and for me, the dreaded Calculus 101. I'm an English lover. Poetry, creative writing, any type of prose feels like heaven to me. But when it comes to anything higher than algebra, I'm a goner. It looks more like hieroglyphics.

Needless to say, that first semester consisted of a lot of 8 a.m. classes, many of which I did not attend. (Partying was much more important to me than learning about the basics of Dr. Freud.) And at the end of the semester, when my parents learned of my 2.0 GPA, they cut me off. We had agreed that as long as I had a GPA higher than 3.25, they would continue to support my tuition. Unfortunately, when they read the report card and noticed it was well under that number, they quickly cut off my funds.

No more money from Mommy and Daddy. I would have to pay for Ball State University on my own.

Thankfully, my dad helped me fill out the forms for the two loans I took on. Lord knows, completing those complicated forms is like taking the SAT. It also felt like I was signing my life away. The government now owned my soul. Well, at least until I paid those puppies off!

The only good thing about school loans is that the government is "nice enough" to allow you to begin making payments after you graduate from school. So for someone like me, who attended college for five years, I didn't receive the bills until I was twenty-two years old.

The first loan was a private loan and not for a crazy amount. It was nothing compared to the total of my government loan. Goodness, that thing was a joke. I could have owned a house by now with the amount I've paid on that thing.

The only good thing about school loans is that the government is "nice enough" to allow you to begin making payments *after* you graduate from school. So for someone like me, who attended college for five years, I didn't receive the bills until I was twenty-two years old.

That's when the freaking out began. Three hundred dollars a month in school loans? Every time I received those bills and wrote out the checks, my heart would sink a little further. All because little ole me had wanted to party all night and skip a few morning classes. Gee, that really paid off, Ash, didn't it?

Although I quickly attained a retail managerial job after graduating (which didn't pay as much as I wished, nor was it anything close to my "dream" job), the bills were piling up, and the amount for even a monthly apartment lease was too much for me to handle. While I could perhaps have found a roommate, all of my girlfriends lived around the state, and the only friends that were close enough were my close guy friends. And there was *no* way my parents would have allowed that to happen!

Living with student loans affected my life dramatically. I had many friends whose parents paid for their education and who were lucky enough to find their dream jobs. These people were also smart enough to not major in English with a creative writing option.

U Chic's Reality Check

According to a recent NBCNews.com article, two-thirds of college graduates leave with a degree and a *large* amount of student loan debt—on average, more than $30,000 per student!

If you are like most college graduates and find yourself facing a pile of student-loan debt, here is some important advice for you:

- **The first thing to do is get organized.** Know how much you owe and to whom. If you took out more than one loan (one from the government and one from a private company), figure out which is at higher rate and, if you can manage, plan on putting more money first toward the loan with the higher interest rate. By paying it off faster, you will end up paying less money overall in the long run.

- **Be sure to make your payments on time.** The last thing you want is to have bill collectors coming after you! Also, if you don't pay on time, your credit score will be dinged, making it harder and more expensive to borrow money in the future. To avoid that scenario, put all of your loan payments on an auto-pay plan so you'll never miss a beat. As an added bonus, many lenders will decrease your interest rate by a certain percentage point if you set up automatic payments.

- **If you do decide to use the auto-pay plan, be sure to make a spreadsheet that indicates what bill is due when, and the specific amount.** That way, you'll never find yourself without enough money in the bank to cover the payments. And of course, budgeting is a must to pull this off!

Having two student-loan payments right out of college was tough, but I did learn a few things from the experience. First, I learned that it was no longer party time; this was real life. Real life comes with hardships, bills, and many 8 a.m. "classes" called jobs (and these you can't blow off!).

While I was happy that my friends' dreams were being fulfilled, deep down, I was a bit envious. They had been out with me on those late nights, had similar hangovers, and had challenging 8 a.m. classes. But they, unlike me, were fortunate enough to have their schooling paid for and were able to do amazing things following graduation, such as traveling around the world, buying the newest tech gadgets, and wearing the cutest, trendiest clothes.

Due to my lack of funds and the amount of school loans I owed, I was unable to travel with friends when they went to Bonnaroo, a musical festival held every year in Tennessee. I'd always wanted to go, and when I had to turn down an invitation from one of my best friends, I felt like my heart had been crushed.

U Chic's Reality Check

What happens if you can't pay? If you find yourself in a situation where you cannot pay your loans—if, for instance, you are unemployed or are terminated from a job—contact the loan provider and ask for a deferment. A deferment excuses you from having to make student loan payments for a set period of time because of a specific condition in your life—such as returning to school, economic hardship, or unemployment. Interest will not accrue on subsidized loans during the deferment period.

If you are working but can't afford to make the full minimum payments, contact the loan provider to work out a payment plan that is do-able. Most companies would rather be paid than not paid at all.

My student loan budget also resulted in me buying a purse from Kohl's rather than the gorgeous leather Coach purse I'd been eyeing for years. Of course, there was no way I had money to buy a new (or used, for that matter) car, resulting in me driving the same car I had all through college, a silver 1996 Dodge Avenger that had more than 175,000 miles on it and was rusted beyond belief.

Having two student-loan payments right out of college was tough, but I did learn a few things from the experience. First, I learned that it was no longer party time; this was real life. Real life comes with hardships, bills, and many 8 a.m. "classes" called jobs (and these you can't blow off!). I also learned how to balance my budget and limit my expenses. I rarely bought things that I wanted and bought things only out of necessity. Bills came first (having bill collectors calling you incessantly is not fun!), and I also came to learn that my parents' tough love was the greatest lesson.

U Chic's Reality Check

Financial advisors often talk about the difference between "good debt" and "bad debt." Good debt, according to these gurus, is your student loans. After all, it's an investment in your future and future earning potential! Bad debt is anything related to that nasty credit-card debt.

If you're financially able to begin paying on your student-loan debt coming out of college in a big way, go for it. It's empowering to be able to take that debt out in a couple of fell swoops, and you'll end up paying a lot less in the long run by paying it off faster. If you're not able to do that, don't sweat it, especially if you are locked into loans that are already at a low interest rate. If you don't have that type of loan—for instance, you have an adjustable private loan rate that keeps ticking up—look into consolidating all of your outstanding debt in one lower-rate loan.

Well, guess what? I recently paid my last student-loan bill, and truly it felt like a weight being lifted off my shoulders. I'm stronger, smarter, and more capable because I did it all on my own!

U Chic's Real-World Essentials—Money Matters

- **So your friends can afford the top-shelf drinks at the hottest new bar in town, but you can't.** Don't sweat it. Invite friends over for dinner. Cooking alone is a bummer, but bringing friends into the kitchen can be a fun new activity, as well as a big money saver.

- **Don't be afraid to say no.** If you really just can't afford tickets to that music festival, drinks at a fancy nightclub, or the weekend trip to California, be honest with your friends. It takes a lot more to end a true friendship than missing out on just one fun-filled weekend.

- **When it's time to settle the bill, it's so easy to swipe that card, right?** Try to keep only one credit card around for emergencies and nothing more. Pay everything else by debit, if you can manage, as it is directly linked to your checking account, limiting you to your bank account balance. If you use a credit card for everyday purchase like groceries or monthly utility bills, try to pay off the balance in full each month. And definitely make your payments on time, because paying late will have a negative impact on your credit score.

- **In choosing a credit card, shop around as you do when on the hunt for a good bargain.** Visit websites like CreditCards.com or Bankrate.com to find cards with the lowest annual percentage rate (APR) and no annual fee. If one also happens to offer cash-back rewards or points, you may have found the perfect one.

- **If you are like most college graduates and find yourself facing a pile of student-loan debt after graduation, be sure to make your payments on time.** The last thing you want is to have bill collectors coming after you! Also, if you don't pay on time, your credit score will be dinged, making it harder and more expensive to borrow money in the future. To avoid that scenario, put all of your loan payments on an auto-pay plan so you'll never miss a beat. As an added bonus, many lenders will decrease your interest rate by a certain percentage point if you set up automatic payments.

Looking for more great advice? Head to www.UChic.com/Diploma-Diaries, where you will find our favorite resources and websites—they come highly recommended by our guide's contributors and editors. Be sure to leave your suggestions as well!

EPILOGUE

Planning for Your Fabulous Future

Well, congrats are in order again. You have made it to the end of the book!

So what do you think? Does the future look bright? It should. You have put a ton of hard work and time into getting to this stage in life, so there is absolutely no reason why this next chapter should be anything but great.

Where you are now may not look exactly like what you planned when you started college all those years ago, but that is completely okay. Life never goes according to plan, and honestly, that's the fun of it. After all, it's a journey, as we said at the start.

We hope that through the essays and tips you've picked up by reading this book, you now have an excellent head start on how to make the most of *your* postcollege life. And if there is any advice I wish I'd had at the beginning of my postcollege life, it is this:

There's no such thing as failure, only life lessons.

You didn't get assigned the project you wanted at work. Your boyfriend dumped you. You got fired from a job. So what? Don't get caught up in obsessing about what hasn't worked out. Some of these things probably weren't right for you anyway.

Now is the time to apply what you've learned to the *future*. I can tell you from experience that your twenties will fly by. Enjoy this stage while it lasts—every success, failure, and occasional surprise that comes your way. Don't waste time dwelling on the past. Today is the start of your future, so embrace it. And while you might not have a clue where you'll end up, today you have a pretty good handle on what matters most to you in life, so make sure that no matter what you do, every moment counts.

acknowledgments

This book is the product of a lot of hard work, support, and passion from a group of people that I love dearly. Thanks must first go to my agent, Loretta Barrett, and my Sourcebooks editor, Stephanie Bowen, for helping me make *Diploma Diaries* a reality. I couldn't have done it without you! Thanks to the team at UChic.com and our fantastic group of contributors. I also want to thank my parents, Jim and Nancy, and my grandfather Bill for their endless support. You have always been there for me, supporting my entrepreneurial endeavors and reminding me that anything is truly possible in this life. Finally, thanks to my lifelong partner and soulmate, Matt. You're a genius in every sense of the word.

contributors

Sara Aisenberg, University of North Texas graduate
Megan Anhalt, University of Southern California graduate
Kara Apel, University of South Carolina graduate
MaryAnn Barone, University of North Carolina–Chapel Hill graduate
Gracie Bialecki, Pomona College graduate
Ashley Cobb, Ball State University graduate
Margaret Darling, Luther College graduate
Emily Diekelmann, Indiana University–Purdue University Indianapolis and Georgia State University graduate
Allison Ehrenreich, Quinnipiac University graduate
Michelle Gaseor, University of Notre Dame graduate
Megan Gebhart, Michigan State University graduate
Hannah Gettleman, University of Illinois graduate
Maggie Grainger, San Diego State University graduate
Jeni Hunniecutt, King College and East Tennessee State University graduate
Marissa Kameno, Quinnipiac University graduate
Jacqueline Loundy, St. John's University graduate
Anna Michels, St. Olaf College graduate
Steph Mignon, Hawaii Pacific University and University of West Los Angeles School of Law graduate
Deborah Musolff, Pennsylvania State University graduate
Kristin Nielsen, University of Nebraska Kearney and Bellevue University graduate
Pamela O'Leary, University of California Berkeley and Claremont Graduate University graduate
Rajul Punjabi, Kean University and Long Island University graduate

Tracey Rector, Indiana University–Purdue University Indianapolis graduate
Emily Roseman, American University graduate
Erica Strauss, Kent State University and Franklin University graduate
Vanessa Thurman, Ohio State University graduate
Brittany Ungerleider, Binghamton University graduate
Jenna Zhu, Swarthmore College graduate